HIS BROTHER'S GRAVE

Joe was shoveling furiously, throwing mounds of dirt around Frank. Within ten minutes Frank was practically covered.

"Joe! Think of what you're doing!" Frank yelled.

But Joe was now foaming at the mouth. His eyes were rolling in their sockets, and he was babbling nonsense words.

Just as Frank was about to be covered, Joe began to shriek insanely. He backed away from the grave as if he were being attacked.

"Finish your job!" the masked man demanded.

But Joe was too far gone.

The masked man aimed his gun at Joe. "I was hoping not to do this, my friend, but you've failed me."

Bracing the gun with two outstretched arms, he fired. . . .

Books in THE HARDY BOYS CASEFILES™ Series

Available from ARCHWAY Paperbacks

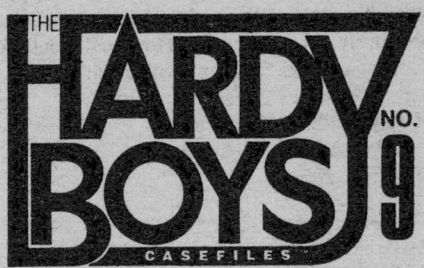

THE GENIUS THIEVES

FRANKLIN W. DIXON

AN ARCHWAY PAPERBACK
Published by POCKET BOOKS • NEW YORK

AN ARCHWAY PAPERBACK *Original*

An Archway Paperback published by
POCKET BOOKS, a division of Simon & Schuster, Inc.
1230 Avenue of the Americas, New York, N.Y. 10020

ISBN: 0-671-63080-6

First Archway Paperback Printing November 1987

10 9 8 7 6 5 4 3 2 1

Printed in the U.S.A.

IL 7+

THE GENIUS THIEVES

Chapter

1

BOOM-BWAP-BADAP! BA-BOOM-BWAP-BADAP!

"Hey, Joe, look at this headline!"

"What? I can't hear you, Frank!"

BOOM-BWAP-BADAP! BA-BOOM-BWAP-BADAP!

"Excuse me! Could you turn that down, please?" Frank Hardy called out as he passed a group of Bayport teenagers who were singing and dancing around a huge box radio. It was blaring out the latest hit by the rock group Frontal Lobe. The pounding drumbeat practically shook the sidewalk.

"NOBODY CAN DO THIS TO ME! OH, BABY, BABY, BABY, LET ME BE! OH, YEAH! OH, NO!"

"I said—" Frank stopped himself. It was no use; no one could hear him. With a roll of his brown eyes and a shrug of his shoulders, he signaled to his brother, Joe, to meet him at the newsstand.

Hands over his ears, Joe Hardy walked toward Frank. He shot an angry glance over his shoulder at the group.

"OO-OOH . . . AA-AAH . . . UHHHHH!"

"I can't believe how loud those idiots are playing that radio!" Joe yelled, hoping the group would hear him.

"Never mind them!" Frank shouted. "I think you'll be more interested in this!" Frank held out a newspaper to his younger brother.

Dzzzzit! Before Joe could read the headline, a sharp electronic noise came out of the radio. The song sputtered. Then, a sudden puff of smoke— and silence.

A couple of passersby broke into relieved applause. The teenagers just stared at the dead radio, dumbfounded.

"Yo, Barry! Some radio—looks like you got ripped off, man!" a skinny kid said.

Frank's eyes widened and shot down to an article on the front page of his paper. Joe couldn't help but snicker at the sight of the kids bent over the radio, scratching their heads.

"Let's get out of here," Frank said. He walked off in the direction of the Hardys' house. Joe followed, fighting back laughter.

Behind them, the street suddenly erupted in commotion. Frank and Joe turned and saw Barry, the owner of the radio, clutching a thin, brown-haired kid by the front of his T-shirt.

"So you think it's funny, wise guy?" Barry was shouting. His thick neck was red with anger. "You want to see something even funnier? Watch my fist!" He jabbed at the thin kid's chest with his free hand. Then he shoved him backward and let go of his shirt at the same time. Stunned, the kid stumbled.

"Come on, Muscles, stand up and fight," Barry said, taunting him as he closed in.

As Barry moved forward, ready to tackle the kid, the kid ducked and ran under Barry's arms and sprinted off.

"Okay, Joe, the show's over!" Frank said. "Let's get out of here!" They headed home.

A few minutes later the brothers jogged up the driveway of the Hardy house and into the living room. Frank laid the newspaper on the coffee table and sat on the couch. Joe couldn't stay still. He paced up and down.

"That guy may have been big, but he couldn't fight. I would have taken him on for the kid."

Frank shook his head and smiled. "Can I finally get you to look at this newspaper? Now, this is important!"

Joe looked at the headline.

WHO'S BLASTING THE BLASTERS?
MYSTERIOUS SHORT-CIRCUITER ON THE LOOSE

"What's the big deal about this?" Joe asked.

"We saw it happen before our eyes!" answered Frank. "The article says that these box radios have been short-circuiting all over the area—for no apparent reason. Police suspect some sort of remote-control jamming device."

"Great! Where can I buy one?"

"Be serious, Joe. If this gets out of hand, who knows what electronic machinery could be tampered with—streetlights, telephones, cash registers—"

Frank was interrupted by a deep voice. "And maybe even bank vaults."

The brothers looked up to see their father, Fenton Hardy, coming down the stairs.

"Hey, Dad," said Frank, "have you seen this story? It's really no joke!"

"No joke intended. I just got a frantic phone call from Sedgwick Trilby, the president of Bayport Bank and Trust. It seems that someone sprang the computer-coded lock on their vault."

"What's that got to do with this story?" asked Joe.

"A possible connection. After all, both crimes could be the work of the same electronics whiz. I'm on my way to the bank now. Want to come?"

The three Hardys climbed into Fenton's car and sped over to the bank.

As they rounded the corner onto Main Street, they saw the hulking old granite building at the far end. Even though the bank had been gutted and renovated on the inside, the facade with the huge marble cornerstone, "Community Savings & Loan 1907" carved into it, had been retained.

Fenton Hardy pulled up in front of the bank, and immediately a tall, balding man in a gray three-piece suit stepped out the front door to meet him.

"Hello, Mr. Trilby," Fenton Hardy said. "I'm sure you remember my sons, Frank and Joe."

Frank thought that Trilby seemed very calm for someone whose bank had just been raided. But it was only an act; his hand vibrated nervously when Frank shook it, and his palm felt clammy.

He wasted no time in ushering the three Hardys through the marble-tiled main room with its high, vaulted ceiling down to the basement.

"It was tough modernizing this old building," Trilby said. "But we managed to tuck the most sophisticated computer system into the existing structure. And we made sure our vault was absolutely theft proof. Or so we thought."

Once in the basement, they walked down a long carpeted hallway at the end of which was a massive steel door, covered with shiny metallic knobs and electronic gauges. It extended twelve feet up to the ceiling.

"Someone broke into *that?*" Joe asked.

"Took two million dollars in cash and shut the door behind him," Trilby said. "Without so much as leaving a fingerprint. The police were here and checked everything out. They didn't say much, but I know Chief Collig—I could tell he was baffled. So I called you in, too, Mr. Hardy."

"There doesn't seem to be any sign of a break-in," Frank said.

"No," Trilby answered, "the vault's lock is hooked up to our mainframe computer. It can only be opened by running a coded program. The program picks the right combination and then chooses a new combination afterward."

"Who has copies of the program disk?" Fenton asked.

Trilby said, "There's only one copy, and I have it. Someone must have cracked the code and made his own disk."

Frank and his father listened while Joe began looking around the area. "You must understand," Trilby said, continuing. "I don't want this to get out. The negative publicity would cause a run on the bank. The theft must remain a secret until the crime is solved. The police have assured us of their discretion."

As Trilby shut the vault, Joe caught a glimpse of something shiny wedged into the crack between the wall and the carpet. He picked it up; it was a brass button attached to a short length of thread. Stamped on the button were the words Chartwell Academy. "Anyone know a crooked preppy who goes to Chartwell?" Joe asked.

Mr. Trilby cleared his throat. "My son Dwight goes there."

Fenton knew this could be trouble and proceeded cautiously. "Do you suppose, Mr. Trilby," he said carefully, "that your son would have any reason to—you know, as some sort of act of rebellion—"

Trilby looked offended. "Absolutely not! I did give him a tour of the bank yesterday, and we did go into the vault. The door is heavy, and Dwight's button may have caught on it while we were struggling to open it." Then he chuckled. "No, my son is devoted to this bank."

Frank and Joe examined all the metal gadgets on the door. There were a lot of sharp edges; the explanation *was* plausible. But not enough to let Dwight—or Mr. Trilby—off the hook.

Suddenly a man in shirtsleeves and a tie raced into the room and said, "Excuse me, sir, there's a problem. Our computers went crazy for a few minutes! You know, nonsense letters—"

"Well, did you fix the problem?" Trilby asked impatiently.

"Uh, yes, sir, but when the computers came back on, they showed a large transfer of money—out of the bank."

"How large?" Trilby demanded.

"Pretty large." The man's eyes glanced nervously around the room—anywhere but at Sedgwick Trilby. "About half a million dollars, sir!"

Chapter

2

"I LOOK LIKE who? Oh, come on, Callie, that's ridiculous—wait a minute, who have you been seeing old movies with?" Frank cradled the phone in his shoulder and stretched out on his bed with a smile on his face.

Just then Joe burst in. "Frank, get off the phone right now! This is important. It's about the bank. And remember, we have to keep this all secret. So tell Callie you'll call her back."

Reluctantly Frank cut short his conversation with Callie Shaw. "All right, what is it?" he asked Joe.

"Who did she think you looked like?" Joe asked with a sly grin.

"Never mind."

"Who?" Joe said, insisting.

Frank turned red as he said, "The guy who played Superman in the movies."

Joe choked back a guffaw and said, "Wishful thinking." Before Frank could respond Joe continued. "Now, get this—Trilby called Dad this morning. Since we saw him yesterday, there's been another big heist at the bank!"

"A break-in?"

"No, it was through the computers again. Just like yesterday. Somebody jams their program so all the screens just show gibberish. It only lasts a minute or so, and when they get back to normal, huge sums of money have been transferred out."

"The thieves have tapped into the program's 'electronic transfer' command," Frank replied.

"You think it's an inside job?" Joe asked.

"Possibly. But someone *could* be doing this from the outside with a modem. That would allow a computer hookup through the phone lines."

Joe's face lit up. "Someone like a very smart computer jock at a prestigious coed boarding school?"

"Are you thinking of Chartwell Academy by any chance?" Frank asked.

"I beat you to it," Joe answered. "I mean, we've seen those movies where whiz kids crack computer codes to find out their grades, start nuclear wars—"

"And Chartwell *is* supposed to be a school for gifted students."

"Right! I think we should investigate. Get a job

there or—or actually enroll! We could transfer for a while. *If* we can get in.''

"It might work," Frank said, scratching his chin. "School's only been on for a week. Maybe Dad can pull some strings and get us in. He could talk to the school here and clear it all.''

They rushed downstairs and found their father just as he was getting off the phone.

"That was Trilby," he said. "He's got a computer expert working on tracing these thefts.''

Frank and Joe explained their idea. Fenton sat down and pondered it for a minute. "I'm not crazy about the idea. But it seems like a good way to investigate this crime," he said. "*If* someone there is involved.''

"Now we're talking!" Joe said. "But how should we do it? If they find out we're from Bayport, whoever's in charge might suspect something.''

Fenton paced around, and then came up with an idea. "After we clear it with your school—and I do say 'after'—how would you feel about becoming a couple of transfer students from Deep River, Montana?''

"Deep River, Montana?" Frank asked, laughing. "Why?''

"An old buddy of mine from the army is a school superintendent there," Fenton answered. "He's always been interested in my detective work. He'd probably be willing to send us fake transcripts, and I know he won't tell a soul.''

10

Joe turned to Frank and said, "Okay, brother, we better stock up on paper and pencils!"

"Not so fast," Fenton said. "There's still one thing that can't be faked."

"What's that?" Frank and Joe asked together.

"The entrance exam. Don't forget, Chartwell is one of the most competitive schools in the country. And we don't know if they have any places."

Joe chuckled smugly. "Hey, no sweat! We can handle the test. I'm sure it'll be a breeze."

"Well, I'm a little less confident than you, Einstein," Frank said. "I think I'll spend some time over at the public library."

"And I have a feeling *you* ought to do a little brushing up yourself, Joe," Fenton added.

"I will," said Joe thoughtfully. "I'll help Frank if he has any questions."

The next day Frank walked up the stairs of the Bayport Memorial Library. The squat, dull building had long been in need of repair; now it was finally being renovated, and the clatter of the workmen surrounded Frank as he wandered around among the shelves.

Before long he sat down with a pile of books and started leafing through them. As he struggled through the geometry review, he thought, This little entrance exam is making me sweat more than any test I've ever taken at Bayport. How do I get myself into these things?

At five o'clock Frank brought his books back to the checkout desk. The librarian, Mr. Douglas, smiled at Frank. "Ah, a well-rounded scholar!" he said. "Perhaps I can suggest a few more, uh, *advanced* texts for you. More appropriate for college preparation."

"No thanks," Frank said. As he walked back out to the parking lot he felt thoroughly depressed; his studying had only just begun. He opened the door of the black van that he and Joe shared. The backseat and floor were totally empty; it was impossible to tell that beneath the carpeted floor was a collection of sophisticated crime-fighting equipment: electronic tracking devices, a mobile phone, disguises, a mini-crime lab with a portable computer, and various ropes and climbing gear.

Frank threw his books onto the backseat and drove home. As he pulled into the Hardys' driveway, Joe ran out the front door.

"Hey, want to go to the movies?" Joe called out.

"What about studying?"

"I've been hitting the books all day. I need a break."

"Any news about Deep River, Montana?" Frank asked.

"Yeah, Dad says everything's set with his friend. He's sent the transcripts to Chartwell. We'll be Frank and Joe Kenyon. And Dad called Chartwell to set up our exam for next Thursday.

They had a couple of transfers, so they have two places. We'll have to be juniors, though. We're as good as in!"

"I hope so," Frank said. It was already Thursday—only a week from the test—and he wondered if he could cram enough in. He gave Joe the van keys. "You go ahead."

"All right," Joe said, shaking his head in disbelief. "But I think you're overdoing the studying bit."

For the next few days Frank pored over his textbooks. Once in a while Joe sat down and leafed through them, too. But he thought he'd have no trouble passing the test.

The exam was to be given in a lecture room at Chartwell Academy, in the town of Kirkland. To get there, Frank and Joe had to drive on back roads they never knew existed. The town was only an hour away, but it seemed like light-years. As they approached Kirkland, the landscape began to change. Neat little suburban houses gave way to sprawling old estates with manicured front lawns, surrounded by tall woods. Some of the houses could barely be seen at the end of long, winding driveways.

"Big bucks, huh?" Joe said.

"I guess so," answered Frank. "I'll bet the school is just like this."

Frank was right. In the distance they saw a tall water tower with the name Kirkland on it. They soon reached the entrance gate. Latin words in gold-painted wrought iron were suspended in an arch between two stone pillars, which flanked the drive. Among the words were *Academia Chartwelliensis*.

"You need to read Latin just to *find* the place," muttered Joe.

Frank drove slowly through the campus as Joe directed him from a map. On both sides of them graceful lindens lined the road. Beyond the trees, neatly dressed students walked to their classes on brick pathways that meandered through wide, freshly cut lawns. The buildings were all made of brick or stone, and it looked as if they'd been there for hundreds of years.

They finally found the right lecture hall and were met by an impatient-looking teacher in a tweed coat. "Ah, the Kenyons, I presume," he said. "Welcome to Chartwell. Please sit. You will have two hours for the exam, and we will call you with the results tomorrow."

Minutes into the exam, Frank realized that his studying hadn't really helped. Numbers, dates, and facts were all jumbled in his mind. At the end, he had to rush to finish the final essay.

Afterward Frank and Joe got into the van and sat still for a moment, trying to recover. "Well, it wasn't too bad," Joe said, speaking first. "I did all the easy questions and then went back."

"Good idea." Frank wanted to kick himself for not thinking of that. Sometimes his brother deserved more credit than he gave him, Frank thought. He sat in stony silence as they drove home.

The next day Frank stayed at home so he wouldn't miss the phone call. Joe disappeared for the day, and when he returned at six o'clock he found his worried brother still close to the phone.

"You've got to loosen up about this, Frank," Joe said. "We don't have anything to prove. Let's keep our minds on the crime."

"Competitive spirit, I guess," Frank said. "I'm not really that nerv—"

Ring-g-g-g! At the sound of the bell, Frank sprang for the phone. Joe had grabbed a bag of pretzels from the cabinet and walked past Frank into the living room to watch TV.

"Hello?" He heard Frank's voice from the kitchen. "Yes . . . oh, great! Thank you . . . What! . . . No, I'll tell him. Goodbye."

Frank returned to the living room. Joe looked up from the baseball game he was watching on TV and said, "What'd I tell you? We made it, right?"

"Sort of," Frank said.

"What do you mean, 'sort of'?" Joe asked, his mouth full of pretzels.

"Well—*I* made it. They want me to start on Monday."

Joe's mouth fell open. "What? I aced that exam! They must have made a mistake!"

"Call them yourself if you don't believe me," Frank said.

As Joe stormed into the kitchen and picked up the phone, Frank stretched out and watched an incredible bases-loaded double play.

That next Monday Frank toted his suitcase through the Chartwell campus on the way to the admissions office. In front of him a couple of leaves from a towering maple tree fell on an old statue of the school's founder, George Howe Chartwell. In front of a dorm, Frank stopped to tuck his striped shirt into his brand-new khaki pants.

For a campus of five hundred students, it seemed awfully quiet, he thought. The kids must have to study all day.

Suddenly the silence was broken by the sounds of shouting above him. Frank looked up. There appeared to be some sort of a fight going on in one of the fourth-floor rooms; Frank couldn't see much from his angle, but he could hear through the open casement window. There was a blood-curdling shriek, and then, as Frank watched in horror, a body came hurtling down from the open window—falling directly at him!

Chapter

3

FRANK THREW HIMSELF off the path and tumbled into a flower bed. He heard the body thud to the ground just beside him.

He sprang to his feet and immediately heard the sound of laughter.

In every dorm window, Chartwell students were slapping one another on the back and laughing hysterically.

Frank rushed over to the limp body and realized what had happened. It was a dummy, dressed in old pants and a wool sweater that said "Winchester School."

Of course, Frank thought. It's football season, and Winchester is their big rival. "Killing" this dummy must be some sort of crazy prep-school tradition.

Frank smiled and waved, all the while wondering what kind of weird place he'd gotten himself into. He brushed himself off as well as he could and continued on to the admissions office. He was met at the door by a student with close-cropped hair and horn-rimmed glasses.

"You must be the transfer student. Kenyon, right?" the student asked, shaking Frank's hand.

"That's right. And you?"

"Pierce. Lloyd Pierce. I'm a junior, too. Also a part-time file clerk here, as part of the work-study program. Congratulations on getting into Chartwell. Don't tell anyone, but I saw your exam. Terrific essay!"

"Thanks," Frank said.

"Too bad about your brother, though," Lloyd said, continuing. "Anyway, let me introduce you to the admissions officers, and they'll give you your class schedule, room assignment, and linens. And if you ever need anything or have any questions, just call me at five-five-five-two-three-oh-one. All the rooms have phones, and the numbers all begin with five-five-five—" Just then his eyes caught the mud stains on Frank's new pants. "And laundry pickup is on Wednesday," he said with a smile.

"Oh! I, uh—lost my footing and fell in a flower bed," Frank said. Lloyd seemed all right. If most of the students are like this, he thought, maybe this place isn't so bad after all.

*   *   *

Frank had arrived too late for his morning classes after going to admissions, but his afternoon classes would begin in an hour and a half. He had plenty of time to drop off his linens and luggage at his dorm, Mansfield Hall.

Mansfield was a sturdy red-brick building with a solid oak-paneled entrance foyer. Frank had had visions of polite, well-dressed students silently grinding away at homework. But the sound of earsplitting rock 'n' roll rang out instead. Frank went in and walked up to the third floor. The loudest rock was coming from his room.

"Nobody can do this to me!"

Frontal Lobe. Just what he needed! With a sigh, he opened the door. Inside, singing and dancing to the music, was a tall, gangly student with an orange headband around a bush of curly hair. Popcorn was spilling out of a large pot on a hot plate in the corner. And in the center of the room, a computer screen flashed a colorful graphics display of a car chase that said "Speed Racer."

"Uh, hello—*hello!*" Frank said, practically shouting above the music.

"Oh, baby, baby, ba—" Suddenly, Frank's roommate stopped singing and saw both Frank and the popcorn. "Uh-oh," he said. With one hand he tried to turn down his cassette player while using the other to save the burning popcorn. Frank put down his suitcase and linens and helped out.

"It's a good thing you weren't Brad," the roommate said. "He doesn't like Frontal Lobe—"

A voice behind them interrupted, " 'Doesn't like' isn't really accurate, Arnie. 'Hates passionately' is closer to the truth."

Frank turned to see a blond, athletic-looking guy wearing tennis whites. "Brad Rogers," he said, extending a hand. "Has my roommate remembered to introduce himself to you?"

"Oh, sorry!" the curly-haired student said. "I'm Arnie Nofziger. You must be Frank."

"That's right. I transferred from—"

"Deep River, Montana," Brad said, cutting in. "Yes, we heard all about you. You know, my ancestors settled Snapoose, the town next to yours. Have you heard of the Snapoose Rogerses?"

"Uh, the name sounds familiar," Frank answered.

"Of course it does. They own practically *everything* there," Brad said with a smirk. "What's your next class, Frank?"

Frank looked at his schedule. "English lit., in about an hour," he said.

"Me, too. Let me shower and change, and then I'll show you around campus before class. Meanwhile, if you happen to be into the wonderful world of calculators and floppy disks, perhaps you and Arnie can find something to talk about."

Brad took his towel and went into the hallway

toward the showers. Arnie held out his pot of popcorn. "Want some?" he asked.

Frank looked at the blackened kernels. "No thanks," he said.

For about five minutes Arnie didn't say a word; he just worked furiously at his computer and ate burned popcorn. Frank made up his empty bed and changed into a clean pair of pants.

Arnie then swung around quickly in his chair and said, "You know, I can show you around campus, too! I know this place better than Brad ever will. Did you know there's a system of tunnels that connects all the buildings on the entire campus? I'm the only one who knows how they all hook up."

"Great," said Frank.

"I can show you the town, too," Arnie continued. "Upperclassmen are allowed limited travel during lunch, which means we can avoid the dining-hall slop and go into Kirkland. There's a Speedy Burger there that has a two-for-one special on Thursdays! And I have a car on campus this semester." A proud grin spread across his face. "I learned how to drive from computer games. My favorite is Speed Racer."

While Arnie was talking, Brad breezed into the room, his hair soaking wet. "Yes, and that's why no one will ride with him," he said.

Arnie stood up and thrust out his chin proudly. "That's not true. You'll come into town with me on Thursday for lunch, won't you, Frank?"

Frank shrugged his shoulders. "Sure, Arnie." He hoped it was the right decision.

When Brad was ready, he walked with Frank through the campus. "That's the arts center, where you meet the most girls," Brad said, pointing to a new marble-and-glass building. "And there's the science laboratory, where you can get the best sleep. The indoor tennis courts—you can usually find me there. And the student lounge, where there's a party Wednesday night. You'll come, of course."

"And the computer terminals?" Frank asked, keeping his mind on the mission.

But Brad wasn't listening. "Oh, yes!" he said. "I almost forgot. Dad and his wife would like to have you for dinner Friday night. They always have to check out my roommates. Dad will send a limo for us, so it'll be easy. You've got to say yes. After bringing Arnie home the last time, I *have* to show up with someone normal!"

Frank finally said yes, and the tour of the school ended at the building where their English class met. Brad and Frank went in and sat down. Frank looked around and was surprised to recognize one other face—the student he'd met at the admissions office, Lloyd Pierce.

The teacher, a Mr. Osborn, was dark-haired with a heavy beard and a potbelly. He peered from behind his wire-rimmed glasses and said, "Now, how many of you have read Shakespeare's *Henry the Fifth, Part One?*" Immediately hands shot up all around the classroom. Frank looked around in disbelief. He'd barely heard of the play—it had taken him half a year to get through *Hamlet* in high school!

"Good. Just about everyone," the teacher said, continuing. "Tell me, how do you see this play in terms of the current American view of nationalism?" Again, students were bursting to try to answer the question, and Frank felt completely lost.

He had the same feeling in social studies, and again in math. By the time he went to his last class, chemistry, he was wondering whether entering Chartwell was really the best way to go about solving this case. After all, they had no proof that the criminals were operating out of Chartwell—they only had that one button as a clue.

The teacher bounded into the room with a confident smile and went straight to the blackboard. "All right," he said. "What I'm about to write will probably look like chicken scratchings, so yell if you don't understand something. My feeling is, if it seems like a stupid question, that means it's probably a good one."

This teacher was friendly and energetic. Frank liked him immediately. At least he didn't make Frank feel like an idiot.

After class the teacher walked up to Frank as he was gathering his books. "Welcome to chemistry class, Frank. I'm Jim Castigan."

"Your name sounds familiar," said Frank.

"Yes, I signed your acceptance letter," Castigan said, the corners of his blue eyes crinkling as he smiled. "You see, I'm also the dean of students, so you can call me if you have any questions at all about Chartwell."

"Forget Chartwell. How about chemistry?" Frank said.

Castigan chuckled. "Come to my office hours on Thursday at eleven A.M.," he said. Then he looked at Frank as if he were sizing him up. "And afterward, if you're interested, I usually take these old bones out to the basketball court."

"Great!" Frank answered. "I'll be there!"

For the next couple of days Frank almost forgot about the computer crimes. It was all he could do to keep up with his classwork. After all, he wouldn't be much use as an undercover detective at Chartwell if he flunked out.

On Wednesday night he was buried in a paperback copy of *Henry V* while Brad napped. At precisely 8:00 an alarm clock rang, and Brad sprang out of bed. "Okay, all rested up and ready to party!" he said, and then slammed Frank's book shut. "Let's put down Shakespeare and shake things up ourselves!"

"Sure," Frank said. I might as well, he thought. This'll be a good chance to meet potential suspects.

They walked to the student lounge, which was

in the basement of the athletic building. Halfway there they could begin to hear music blaring and students laughing and talking.

Inside the packed room Frank recognized quite a few of the students from his classes. In the middle, some were dancing, and along the walls, others sat or tried to squeeze by one another. As they got themselves sodas from a machine, a thin guy with a checked shirt and old jeans came up to Brad.

"Hey, Brad," he said. "Have you seen Arnie?"

"No. Oh, Jed, this is our new roommate, Frank Kenyon. Frank, meet Jed Wilson." Frank looked hard at Jed—he had the feeling he'd seen him before. But he couldn't remember when or where.

Jed barely nodded at Frank before turning back to Brad. "Well, tell him I debugged our new program disk, okay?"

"Sure, Jed," Brad said. As Jed went back into the crowd, Brad murmured to Frank, "Definitely the other side of the tracks, if you know what I mean. His father fills potholes for a living."

Just then, out of the corner of his eye, Frank saw a hand reaching up for Brad's back pocket. "Watch it, Brad!" he shouted.

Brad spun around and looked down at a group of students sitting on the floor. One of them was pulling his hand away. He gave Brad a broad grin.

"Trilby, you crook!" said Brad, laughing. "You'll *never* have enough money!"

Trilby. This must be the banker's son Dwight, Frank thought. Brad slapped the guy playfully on the back and walked away. Obviously, they were just kidding around. But Frank kept an eye on Dwight Trilby. He had a jutting jaw and slick, jet-black hair, and he was bragging loudly about something he had done in football practice. Frank noticed immediately that Dwight's blazer had a button missing.

Dwight did a double-take when he noticed Frank staring at his jacket. "Checking out the merchandise? Let me know if there's something you like," he said sarcastically. His friends laughed nervously.

This guy looks like trouble, Frank thought. But out loud he said, "Thanks, I will." Then he turned to follow Brad.

"Hey! New boy! I haven't finished talking to you!"

Frank's jaw tensed. Cool it, he said to himself. The last thing you need right now is a fight with your major suspect.

He faced Dwight. "Look, I'm—" he began. But he got no further. One of the dancers gyrating behind him chose that moment to try a triple spin. The kid fell against Frank, making him stumble forward. Some of Frank's soda sloshed out of the can—and splashed down into Dwight's face. "Oh, great," Frank groaned softly.

With an enraged roar, Dwight rose to face Frank. And rose—and rose some more. The room fell silent, except for the thumping dance music. And Frank found himself staring up at Chartwell Academy's star six-foot-four linebacker.

"Sorry! It was an accident!" Frank said, although he knew it wouldn't do much good.

With his left hand, Dwight grabbed Frank's arm and hauled him forward so that their noses were almost touching. "It didn't look like an accident from *my* perspective," he growled.

"Listen, I really don't want to fight," Frank said.

"Oh, no? Well, that's a shame, because *I* do." And Dwight's right fist shot forward to connect with Frank's jaw.

Chapter

4

FRANK HAD SEEN the blow coming, so he was able to twist a little and take it at an angle. When it hit, he let his head snap back, so that Dwight's fist only glanced along his jaw. Still, the impact made his ears ring.

Frank sagged. Dwight grinned and shifted his hold for another strike. As he felt the movement, Frank brought his own hand up and let it fall in a slicing karate blow to Dwight's wrist.

With a yell, Dwight let go of Frank. As Frank jumped backward, he saw the murderous expression on the football player's face. There was no way Dwight would let him go now, Frank decided. He'd just have to try to wind it up with as little damage as possible. He sighed. "Oh, well, I tried," he muttered as they squared off.

Dwight lunged at Frank with a powerful left

jab. Frank blocked the punch with his right arm. Then Dwight came back with a strong right. Frank ducked skillfully and Dwight's fist sliced the air. The force of his own weight made him fly into the crowd.

"Knock it off, Trilby!" Brad called out, and he tried to grab Dwight. But Dwight was steaming, and he threw off Brad's grip in one powerful motion. Frank waited for Dwight across the room in a karate stance.

"Oh, I hate these martial-arts types," Dwight said under his breath. "I think you'd do better to try prayer instead!" With that, he hurled himself toward Frank in a flying tackle.

When Frank saw two hundred and fifteen pounds of Grade-A American muscle leaping toward him, he did the only sensible thing. He gracefully stepped out of the way.

Dwight Trilby went sailing headfirst past Frank and into the jukebox. The speakers gave out a ripping noise as the needle scraped along the record inside the machine.

The students all rushed to surround Dwight as he lay motionless on the floor. "Is he all right?" someone asked.

"Is *he* all right?" said Brad. "What about the jukebox?"

Brad and some of his friends brought Dwight outside so he could get some fresh air. A female student watched them take Dwight away and looked admiringly at Frank. "Not many people get the best of ol' Ironsides Trilby," she said.

Frank gave her a humorless grin. "Yeah, I can see it's going to do wonders for my reputation around here." This was going to make it ten times harder to investigate Dwight Trilby!

He strode outside with Brad, where Dwight was coming to. Mr. Castigan had been called to the scene and was standing over Dwight.

"Kenyon!" Castigan called out as he looked up from Dwight. "Are you responsible for this?"

"In a sense, sir," Frank answered.

"With all due respect, sir," Brad put in, "I think the jukebox did most of the damage." He grinned at them both and then sauntered back inside.

Mr. Castigan looked angry for a second and then walked closer to Frank. He winked slyly and said under his breath, "Trilby had it coming. But stay away from him next time, okay? He's been acting pretty strange lately."

Frank thoughtfully agreed and walked back to Mansfield Hall.

Back in Bayport, Joe and Fenton Hardy were picking up new clues in the Bayport Bank and Trust thefts. On Monday and Wednesday there had been two more computer money transfers. Both fit the pattern of the first crimes, except that they were for smaller amounts of money now.

By Thursday morning Mr. Trilby's patience

was wearing thin. "I don't *care* if you're a board member," he shouted into the phone. "I *can't* freeze all the money in the bank! I'll have to explain everything to the customers, and they'll *all* pull their money out. Don't worry, I've got an expert working on it—"

At that moment, Mr. Trilby's secretary ushered Joe and Fenton into his office. The banker wearily said goodbye to the board member and hung up the phone.

"We came as soon as we got your call, Mr. Trilby," Fenton Hardy said.

"Yes, yes, I'm sure," Trilby said hurriedly. "I have some good news, fellows. My computer expert, Waldo McKay, may have cracked the case."

Joe and Fenton sat down to listen. "These computer pirates have been extremely crafty. They've been waiting until the precise moment that the computer system is on the brink of over-loading—which usually happens around lunch-time, when the bank is busiest. Then they strike. Something seems to seize the computer. We don't know what."

"So it appears to be like any other temporary malfunction," Mr. Hardy said.

"That's right," Mr. Trilby said. "And so much memory is being tied up in the computer that it's almost impossible to trace the source."

"What happens when the computers come back on?" Joe asked.

"That's where Waldo comes in," Trilby said. His eyes were flashing with an optimism Joe hadn't seen before. "The pirates have been so careful in encoding their transfers that Waldo says it'll take months to figure out where all the stolen money went—all except for the last theft."

"He traced that one?" Joe said excitedly.

"He sure did," Trilby answered, rubbing his hands. "Either the crooks blundered or Waldo was on the ball, but he traced a transfer of twenty-five thousand dollars to a nearby account. Immediately after that the crooks must have gotten wise, because the money was transferred out of *that* account to someplace he couldn't trace, possibly overseas."

"What was the first account?" Joe asked.

"A small electronics firm based in Kirkland. The company's name is Chip-Shape, Inc."

"Did Waldo get the name of the owner?" Fenton asked.

"I was in the process of finding that out when you arrived, gentlemen," he said. He turned back to his computer; the screen was lit up with a list of names that looked like the Yellow Pages. "I've accessed a list of local Kirkland businesses. Now let's call up 'Electronics'—" He punched a couple of keys. "And now, 'Kirkland'—" A couple more keys. "Here it is! Chip-Shape!"

He pressed two more keys and the screen glowed with information about Chip-Shape.

Trilby read aloud from the screen: " 'Small electronic parts, computer software—' "

"That makes sense," said Joe.

" 'Mail order, limited retail, sales eleven thousand two hundred and fifty dollars,' " Trilby continued. "Hmm, a small company. Let's see, 'Founder, owner, and president . . .' "

Trilby stopped reading and looked as if he'd seen a ghost.

"Who is it, Mr. Trilby?" Fenton asked. "Someone you know?"

Trilby kept staring at the screen and said softly, "It's a friend of my son's at Chartwell—Jed Wilson."

It took no time for Joe to call Frank and give him the news. Frank was stunned.

"He *owns* a company?" said Frank. "I met him last night! He's younger than you are!"

"Well, you know, these computer geniuses start early," Joe replied over the phone. "His parents probably have custody of the money."

"Okay, thanks. I have to run and meet a teacher for office hours," Frank said.

"Office hours?" Joe was surprised. If *Frank* needed help with classwork, he was kind of glad he didn't get in to Chartwell.

"It's unbelievable, Joe. They're teaching stuff we have never learned at Bayport. I feel like I'm in college."

"I figured that would happen," said Joe with a

little triumph in his voice. "That's why I purposely messed up that entrance exam!"

"Right." Frank shook his head, hung up, and raced over to Mr. Castigan's office. After a half hour of discussing chemistry, he and Castigan grabbed a basketball and ran out to the courts near one of the school parking lots.

For a forty-year-old man, Castigan wasn't bad. What he lacked in quickness, he made up for in rebounding strength and dead-accurate jump shots. After fifteen minutes, the score was tied 8–8.

"Time out!" Castigan called. "You're wearing me out, Kenyon! Taking advantage of a tired old man!"

Frank laughed. "Give me a break, Mr. Castigan! I never thought anyone your age could block my lay-ups!"

"Well, don't put me in a nursing home yet! Okay, your ball. Next basket wins."

Frank put the ball into play. He dribbled to the top of the key, with Castigan close behind him. Then he faked left, dribbled behind his back, moved to the baseline, and jumped. The ball flew out of his hands, but only traveled about two inches before Castigan whacked it out toward the foul line.

"Pretty good move, Castigan!" Frank said, panting.

Now Castigan had the ball. As he dribbled it, he challenged Frank, face-to-face. In both of their eyes was fierce concentration. Frank darted his hand out for the ball. Castigan bounced it out of his reach. Frank retreated. Castigan looked right but moved left. Frank was thrown off balance but scrambled to follow Castigan as he darted toward the basket.

Neither of them noticed the battered old sedan that was coming close to them, swerving all over the parking lot at top speed.

Castigan went under for the lay-up. Frank caught up with him and jumped up to block the shot. Castigan barreled into Frank, and Frank went tumbling out of bounds—right into the path of the speeding sedan!

Chapter

5

FRANK SPRAWLED ON the ground, two feet from the careening car.

"Look out!" Mr. Castigan shouted.

Screeeeech! The sedan skidded to a stop inches from Frank's face. He rolled out of the way and sprang to his feet.

The noon sun glared off the tinted windshield, making it impossible to see who was driving. Somebody's on to me, Frank thought, and he braced himself to run. The car would probably try to pull out of the parking lot—or come after him again.

Instead, the driver's door opened. He's probably got a gun! Frank dove onto the ground behind the passenger side. He watched for the driver's feet under the car. He figured the only thing he could do was keep the car between himself and the killer.

The driver's feet swung out and hit the ground. Red high-top sneakers.

"Wow! Still stops on a dime, eh, Mr. Castigan—just like the car in Speed Racer! Hey, where's Frank?"

Frank recognized the voice. He rose and looked over the car.

It was Arnie.

Castigan's arms were folded tightly, and he looked at Arnie with a mixture of shock and relief. "Young man, do you have any idea—"

Arnie slammed his door shut and saw Frank staring at him from the other side. "Kenyon!" he said. "What is this, some sort of hide-and-seek? Did you forget about lunch today?"

Frank saw Mr. Castigan's mouth open wide in disbelief. Arnie looked from one to the other and scratched his head. "Is something wrong?"

"Uh, Arnie," Frank said, leaning his elbows on the vinyl roof, "I'll go with you under two conditions: that I get behind the wheel, and that we have a long talk—about how you learned to drive."

Arnie agreed, and the two of them drove off—slowly—to the Speedy Burger.

That night Frank began his investigation. He waited until midnight, when most of the students and faculty were asleep, and then sneaked out to go into the administration building.

The autumn wind rustled the ivy on the building walls as he passed. There were no lights inside the building, and no guards.

After four days in the school, Frank had learned all about its security there—or lack of it. Crime was practically unheard of at Chartwell, except for the occasional sabotaging of science projects and stealing of homework. The campus was patrolled by two guards, one of whom seemed to spend most of his shift napping in the arts center.

Frank crept up the front stairs. To his amazement, the door was open. They must really trust one another here, he thought. He walked up the two flights to the registrar's office and peeked through the glass door. The light of the moon shone into the room and lit up a row of four-drawer file cabinets. Next to the cabinets was a photocopy machine and a computer. This door was locked, but Frank opened it easily with his plastic student ID card.

He walked in, took out his pocket flashlight, and turned on the photocopy machine. The sudden, mechanical *whirrr* was startling in the silence. Frank hoped it wouldn't attract attention.

Next he found the file drawer marked *W.* He pulled it open and riffled through the files until he saw "Wilson, Jed." He read through the file and made copies of some papers. Then he returned the file to the drawer and went over to the computer.

He flicked it on and accessed a student list. Good, he thought, they describe the students' interests here. I can find out who all the computer whizzes are, and then get a printout. He pressed a few keys, trying to figure out how exactly to do it.

Suddenly Frank thought he heard footsteps. He froze. There were only two possibilities of escape: jumping out the window to the ground two stories below or going into the next office through a connecting door.

Choosing the less painful route, Frank started for the door—just as the light flicked on in the office. "Okay, hold it right there!" a voice bellowed. Frank turned helplessly around. A man stood with his right hand on the light switch. His face was blocked by the open top drawer of the file cabinet, but Frank could see by his uniform that he was a custodian. Just my luck, Frank thought.

The man let go of the light switch and pushed in the file drawer, revealing his face.

Frank's eyes popped open. "Joe!" he cried. "What are *you* doing here?"

"Well, I had to get into Chartwell *somehow*," Joe said. His blond hair was sprayed jet black, and he was wearing a thin false mustache. "They had an opening for a custodian in the graveyard shift. I applied today under a false name, and they hired me on the spot." He smiled proudly. "I figured it had to be you in here. Did I scare you?"

"Of course not," Frank replied. "Until I saw that hideous disguise, that is."

"Don't worry. The hair color is strictly temporary."

"All right, there's no time to waste. Shut off the light, stop talking, and help me find some information."

Together they went over to the computer and Frank hit a couple of keys. While they waited for the information to show up, Frank said, "Look at these copies of Jed Wilson's file."

Joe took the papers off the photocopy machine and grabbed his own flashlight. Before he could read anything, they both heard more footsteps in the hallway.

"You didn't get Dad a job here, too, did you?" asked Frank.

"No!" said Joe. "Quick, let's get out of here!"

"Go ahead! First I've got to cover all traces— I'll be right behind you!"

Joe disappeared through the door that led to the next office. Frank first turned off the computer and then the photocopy machine. He ran to the inside door and stepped into the other room. Quickly he glanced back into the registrar's office to double-check.

And there, sitting all alone on top of an empty

table, was his student ID card. He had left it there when he first came in.

Great detective methods, he said to himself and raced over to the table. He grabbed the card, stuffed it into his pocket, and ran back to the side door.

"Stay right where you are, young fella!" Frank turned to face a plump, elderly man in a uniform, who looked more afraid than Frank was. Frank recognized him as the guard who liked to take naps. In one of his waking moments, he must have seen the office light when Joe had flicked it on.

"Wh-wh-what are you doing in here?" the man sputtered. "Are you a student?"

"Yes. Isn't this the student lounge?" Frank asked with a smile.

But the guard was in no mood to joke. "I'm afraid you'll have to follow me," he said.

They walked into the hallway at the same time that Joe had decided to sneak out of the office next door.

The guard gasped and shouted, "Stop, you!" Joe fled the stairway—where he was met by another man! The man grabbed him by the arm and brought him back down the hallway toward Frank.

In the shadows Frank didn't recognize the man. He said, "I must say I'm extremely disappointed in both of you." The voice was familiar.

Then the man snapped on the hall light. It was Castigan.

Pulling Joe roughly, Castigan walked up to the old guard and said, "Thank you for notifying me about this, Mr. Lucas. And thanks for investigating it alone before I arrived." He turned to Frank and said, "If you're going to snoop around, my young friend, you'd stand a better chance of succeeding with the lights off."

"Mr. Castigan—"

"As for *you*," he said to Joe, "you are, of course, fired, effective immediately. And you'd be wise never to be seen on this campus again." Then he turned to Frank with a look of both anger and pity. "I can't tell you how sad this makes me, Frank—"

"Please let me explain—"

"You have nothing to explain to me," Mr. Castigan cut Frank off again. Frank was a little surprised at his abrupt change of manner. Why won't he even give me a chance? Frank wondered. I guess he's not quite the guy I thought he was.

Mr. Castigan continued speaking. "You'll have to take it up tomorrow morning with a tribunal of your fellow students. That's the way it's done here at Chartwell. Mr. Lucas, let's escort these two gentlemen out of the building."

The tribunal was arranged for ten o'clock the next morning. Frank walked into a small classroom to find seven students behind a long, wooden table—four of them were guys and three girls. As they stared at him with serious expressions, he sat in a chair facing them. He noticed the large clock above their heads. It seemed to be ticking awfully loud—almost as loud as his heartbeat.

In the center was Lloyd Pierce, the student Frank had met in the admissions office on Monday. Today he seemed considerably less friendly. He rose and said, "Frank, this is a court of your peers, in accordance with Chartwell rules. I am the presiding judge." He indicated the students to his immediate right and left. "My two counselors are Stu Goldman and Ty Farnsworth, Junior. It has been reported to us . . ."

This is right out of a bad movie, Frank thought as Lloyd droned on.

"Do you understand the charge?" Lloyd asked at the end.

"Yes, sir," Frank replied. "I mean, yes!"

"Do you have an explanation?"

Frank's alibi was all ready. He tried to appear cheerful and relaxed. "I'm really embarrassed, Lloyd," he said. "Last night as I went to bed, I realized I had no idea where my eight-o'clock class was being held this morning. I thought it might be posted on a list outside the administration building."

"It's never done that way," Stu said.

"Well, I found that out from Joe, the new

43

custodian, who was walking into the building to clean it. He told me the lists were in the hallway, so I went in with him.''

"But the registrar's office is on the third floor," Ty said.

"Right. Joe said he was going up to clean that office. And when I heard that, my curiosity got the better of me. I sneaked up after him and saw that he had left the office door open. When I went inside, Joe had already gone through into another office." Frank blushed and shrugged his shoulders. "And, yes, I'll admit it—I was *dying* to see what the evaluators wrote on my admissions file."

At that, a couple of the students smiled and nodded their heads. They sympathized—obviously, some of them had had the same idea themselves. Good, it's working, Frank thought.

Lloyd stood up once again. "Thank you, Frank," he said. "Unfortunately, it seems that the custodian was there illegally, too—although you couldn't have known that. Now please wait here while the tribunal recesses. We will decide on a penalty to recommend to the administration."

Frank waited while they all went into another room. He felt confident his alibi had worked. He'd probably get off with a reprimand.

The tribunal returned after about ten minutes. Lloyd Pierce came in last, with Stu and Ty, and read from a piece of paper. "Frank, as we all know, grades are important in school. But more important is what we learn about right and wrong."

Oh, just get on with it, Frank thought.

"It is always sad when a student shows that he or she does not understand this difference and is incapable of living up to the standards of Chartwell Academy. Your actions cannot be condoned.

"Therefore, by majority vote, we have decided to recommend expulsion to the Chartwell administration."

Frank's stomach sank. The mission had just gone up in smoke.

Chapter

6

As THE SEVEN students left the room, Frank felt stunned. The investigation was back to ground zero.

Slowly he stood and picked up his books. "Guess I won't be needing these anymore," he muttered out loud.

"Oh, don't be so sure," a friendly voice said. Frank looked around and saw a sandy-haired girl in the doorway; she was smiling at him. He recognized her as one of the students on the tribunal.

"I'm Sarah Waterbury," she said. "I believed you. I think it's rotten they decided that way—give them a little power and they think they're the Supreme Court. You look like you're taking it pretty hard."

"Well, those are the breaks." Frank sighed as

he walked past her to the door. "I'm sure you'd feel the same way."

Sarah laughed. "No, not at all. You don't know this school, Frank. This whole thing is usually just a show—makes the students feel important. The administration *never* takes these recommendations seriously. Besides, they're too afraid to expel students because of what their parents might do—the rich ones would stop donating money to the school!"

"No kidding," Frank said. "So you think they'll let me stay?"

"You'll get a lecture from Mr. Castigan, a slap on the wrists, and they'll send you off to class and have something to gossip about at the faculty dinner."

She cocked her head slightly, and the ends of her mouth curled up in a quirky smile. There was something about this girl, Frank thought. She had a kind of strength and sense of humor that he found attractive. If he weren't going out with Callie, he'd want to get to know her better. And from the look in her eyes, he could tell she was thinking the same thing about him.

Come on, now, Frank, he said to himself. Don't lead her on. "Thanks, Sarah, that really makes me feel a lot better," he said. Then he looked at his watch. "Whoops! I'm going to be late for math. See you!"

"Wait!" she said. "You've got five whole minutes. I'll walk with you. I have to go to physics."

Together they strolled through campus. Frank tried to walk at a brisk pace, but Sarah wanted to chat.

"Aren't you in my English class with Mr. Osborn?" she asked.

"Yes."

"Are you prepared for that Shakespeare test Monday?"

"Ha!" Frank said. "It took me three days just to get through *Henry the Fifth*. Now I have to figure out what all the words mean!"

Sarah laughed. "It's not so bad as you think. Why don't you come over to study with me tomorrow?"

That definitely sounded like a line. Frank could see Callie's disapproving eyes. But he was so lost in the course, and Mr. Osborn didn't do anything to make it less confusing.

"Maybe I will, Sarah," he said as they entered the building. "*If* you're right and they don't kick me out."

"Great!" Sarah said with a broad smile. "My room is Van Cott twenty-one. I'll be starting at ten in the morning. 'Bye!" She gave him a quick wave and skipped up the first-floor stairs.

"You have reached the residence of Fenton and Laura Hardy. We can't take your call right now, but at the sound of the tone, pl—"

Frank slammed the phone down in frustration. No one was picking up on his and Joe's private line *or* his parents' phone. He'd been trying to call ever since he had gotten back from his last class. Where could they be?

"Parents out painting the town red, eh?" Brad said from his corner of the room. "I know what *that* feels like. At least I know mine are home tonight; they have to entertain you for dinner. Cheer up, the car should be arriving soon. The food'll be great, even if we do have to sit and discuss our futures for two hours."

Honk! Honk! Brad looked out the window at the limo. "Okay, let's go!" he said, running out of the room. Frank followed and locked the door behind him.

In front of the dorm was a shiny black stretch limo. A man wearing a uniform stood holding the back door open. Brad was already in the backseat. "Frank, this is Oscar," he called out. "Oscar, Frank. Now let's get out of here before someone steals a hubcap!"

As they drove through the quiet countryside, Frank tried to watch the TV in the backseat, but Brad kept flipping from channel to channel.

Before long the rural calm gave way to honking taxicabs and stop-and-go traffic. Oscar drove them over a brightly lit bridge and into New York City. Frank looked out the window at block after block of apartment buildings that stretched forty floors into the sky.

The car pulled into the circular driveway of a huge glass-and-steel building with fountains lit up in front. Brad led Frank into the mirrored elevator. A uniformed elevator operator brought them up to a floor labeled "PH."

"That stands for penthouse—forty-seventh floor," Brad said. "Hope you're not afraid of heights."

They took a left out of the elevator. At the end of the hall, a woman in an apron called out, "Hello, boys!" A spicy, welcoming smell followed her through the open door to greet them.

"Hi," Brad said, sniffing the air. "What's cooking?"

"Aren't you going to introduce your friend, Bradley?"

Frank smiled and stuck out his hand. "Hello, Mrs. Rogers. I'm Frank Hardy."

The woman looked blank and Brad guffawed. "Frank, this is Amelia—she's our cook. Come on, I'll introduce you to the folks."

Just then a tall, silver-haired man in a navy-blue blazer appeared in the front hallway. Next to him was a trim, elegantly dressed woman. "Ah, boys, you're here! Marvelous!" he said. "Hello, Frank, I'm Malcolm Rogers, and this is Brad's stepmother, Joan."

"Pleased to make your acquaintance," Frank said.

"Likewise," Mrs. Rogers said. "Do come in and make yourself at home."

Home was the last place this looked like, Frank thought. More like a museum. The walls were covered with huge framed oil paintings, each one separately lit. Porcelain vases flanked the sofa, and a collection of antique figurines was displayed in a specially designed cabinet.

In a few minutes they all sat down to eat in the Rogerses' dining room, which had an incredible view of the river.

"I hear you're from Deep River, Montana, Frank," Mr. Rogers said after they had finished their crabmeat mousse.

"Born and raised there," Frank said as Amelia served their salad course.

"We have family in Snapoose, you know."

"Uh-huh. That's what Brad says."

"Yes. Tell me, is your family the Kenyons who own the livery stable?" Mr. Rogers asked.

"Uh, right! That's us!" Frank said and smiled.

During the main course of swordfish, the conversation moved on to school and what Frank planned to do when he graduated.

"So, what do you do, Mr. Rogers? For a living, I mean," Frank asked later.

Mr. Rogers chuckled. "Oh, not much of anything. Consultant to a few small companies, board member of a couple of banks. You know, Clairmont Bank, Bayport Bank and Trust—"

This wasn't something Frank expected to hear. "No kidding! I just opened my first checking account there—in the Bayport Bank. Do you think it's a good bank?"

"Why, yes, of course," Mr. Rogers answered.

"Safe? Up-to-date?" Frank went on questioning Mr. Rogers, watching for his reaction. "I understand they have a top-notch computer system."

"They do. It's the best," Mr. Rogers said, clipping his words. Then he abruptly raised his voice slightly and spoke toward the kitchen, "Amelia! We're ready for dessert now!"

He knows something. I can tell by the way he's acting, Frank thought. He excused himself from the table and looked at Brad. Brad pointed down the hall where the bathroom was.

On his way, Frank passed by Mr. Rogers's study. Piles of papers littered the desk. On some of them, he could see the words "Bayport Bank and Trust." Looking up and down the empty hallway first, he slipped inside the room.

Quickly and quietly, Frank riffled through a stack of computer printouts, looking for clues. But the columns of numbers just looked like gibberish. Finally he saw something at the bottom of the pile that caught his eye—a letter from Mr. Trilby, dated the day before. He pulled it out.

And, instantly, was aware of someone breathing behind him.

Frank spun around to see Oscar, the chauffeur, standing in the doorway. In his hand was a gun.

Chapter

7

FRANK DROPPED DOWN behind the desk. "Don't shoot! I'm Frank, a friend of the family!"

Oscar looked at him closely in the dimly lit room and put his gun down. "So you are," he said. "Terribly sorry, Frank, I didn't mean to scare you."

"That's all right," Frank replied, getting back onto his feet. "Do you always carry a loaded thirty-eight with you?"

"Oh, no, it's not loaded," Oscar said. "You see, Mr. Rogers requires that I carry it. He claims there's been a series of break-ins in the building lately, though in my opinion, there's no need for bullets—"

"Yes, well, we don't get paid for our opinions,

do we, Oscar?'' came Mr. Rogers's voice from the doorway.

"Pardon me, sir!" Oscar said.

"You may go now, Oscar."

"Of course."

"And, Oscar—"

"Yes, sir?"

"Load the gun!"

As Oscar scurried out the door, Malcolm Rogers glared menacingly at Frank.

"So, Mr. *Kenyon*," he said, practically spitting out his words. "You have an interest in the Bayport Bank and Trust? In the computer system?"

Frank grinned. "Guess my curiosity got the better of me, sir."

"I see. Well, *I* am curious myself." He slammed the study door and slowly approached Frank. "Who are you?"

"You know who I am, Mr. Rogers. I'm Frank Kenyon."

"Of the Deep River Kenyons, eh?"

"That's right."

"The Deep River Kenyons *who don't exist!*"

"Hey, that's my mother and father you're talking about—" Frank said, protesting.

"Spare the theatrics, whoever-you-are," Mr. Rogers said, interrupting. "I had my people in Snapoose run a check on you. No one's ever heard the name Kenyon in Deep River. Now tell me what you're doing here!"

Frank looked squarely into his eyes. "You seem pretty desperate, running a check on your son's roommate. Are you afraid of something?" He reached for the pile of Bayport Bank and Trust papers.

The veins in Mr. Rogers's neck were popping out. "Out of my house!" he said, on the verge of exploding. "You will leave quietly. I will tell my family that you had a bad reaction to the fish and that you had to be sent home. Bradley will spend the night here. What happened between you and me is never to be mentioned to Bradley. It will disturb his concentration at school. Is that understood?"

"If you say so, sir." Frank shrugged, gazing steadily at Malcolm Rogers. This investigation was *not* going like clockwork. Not at all.

Rogers grabbed him by the collar and moved his face to within inches of Frank's. "I'll be keeping tabs on you at Chartwell, Mr. *Kenyon*. And you'd be wise not to have any contact with the Bayport Bank and Trust."

He let go, and Frank brushed himself off and walked into the hallway and out of the apartment.

"Next stop is Short Neck!"

The bus driver's voice woke Frank. The ride back to Kirkland was far different from the limo ride. The bus had stopped at just about every small depot along the way and jangled over every rutted road.

Frank thought about Malcolm Rogers. Was he guilty of swindling his own bank? He wished he could have read the letter from Trilby.

After an hour and a half the bus pulled up to Chartwell's front gate. Frank was the only person to get off. In the darkness he noticed the outline of a large car or truck down the road. As he started through the gate, he heard a motor rev up. He looked back and saw the vehicle move slowly toward him with its headlights flashing.

Frank could see the newspaper headlines right then: "Wandering Preppy Killed by Night Stalker." He took off running into the campus.

A whistle pierced the air and then a shout followed. "Frank! It's me!"

Frank turned to see that the mysterious vehicle was a van—Frank and Joe's van!

"Joe?"

"No—Santa Claus," Joe said. "I'm a little early." Frank noticed that Joe's mustache was gone but the black spray was still in his hair.

"Where have you been?" Frank asked.

"You took the question right out of my mouth! I've been trying to call your room on our mobile phone for an hour!"

"It's a long story. But we have another suspect. Guy named Rogers—board member of the bank. His son is one of my roommates."

"Great," said Joe. "Maybe he's in cahoots

with Jed Wilson. Dad and I analyzed Wilson's records and dug up a lot of info about him.''

"Do we have a case?"

"You bet. He's a real go-getter. Comes from a poor family in Rockchester. But the guy's a computer genius, so Chartwell gave him a full scholarship. He set up his own electronics and software company at age sixteen. A company that has been showing steadily increasing profits these past few months.

"Not to mention the deposit and withdrawal into his company's account of the twenty-five thousand dollars that was stolen from Bayport Bank and Trust last week."

"Looks like an open-and-shut case to me," Joe said.

"No, there are still too many loose threads," Frank answered. "Let me show you my notes. Come on, I'll drive the van into campus. You lay low—someone may recognize you."

"Not necessarily," Joe said. He reached into the backseat for a red, curly wig, which he slipped over his black-sprayed hair. Frank just looked at him blankly.

"It's the only disguise I could get on quick notice," Joe said, shrugging his shoulders.

"Terrific. Now you've gone from Dracula to Little Orphan Annie."

Frank drove slowly to the parking lot near his dorm and parked the van next to Arnie's car.

Then he and Joe walked along the darkened pathway to Mansfield Hall. They entered through the basement.

"You live in this dump?" Joe whispered. "It smells like a locker room."

Frank rolled his eyes and led Joe to the back stairwell. They took the stairs up to the third floor, where a different smell greeted them. Burning food. Frank and Joe looked down the hallway to see smoke puffing out from beneath Frank's door. Crazy Arnie and his popcorn again, Frank thought. At that moment the smoke alarm began shrieking.

Joe started running for the room, but Frank pulled him back.

"What are you doing, Frank?" Joe asked, furious. "Maybe someone's in there!"

Frank stood still, sniffing the air. "Wait a minute!"

"Come on, I was kidding about the locker-room smell—" But Joe caught a whiff of something unexpected, too. "I think I smell gasoline. We'd better move!" he said. "If this thing spreads, we're all in trouble!"

Joe ran to the door of Frank's room. Frank took out his keys. "We don't need them," said Joe, reaching for the doorknob. "It's open."

"Careful of the smoke!" Frank warned Joe. "Push the door open and stand back!"

As Joe threw the door open, smoke billowed

out into the hallway. From on top of the door, a bucketful of clear fluid cascaded down.

Frank took one sniff of the air and lunged for his brother, pulling him back out of the way. "Get back, Joe!" he shouted. "We just found that gasoline!"

Chapter

8

THE BUCKET CLATTERED to the floor, spilling liquid all over.

"What the—" Joe's eyes narrowed.

"Did you get any on you?" Frank asked.

"A little splashed on my wig—"

"Take it off and throw it up the hallway. Let's go!" Frank leaped across the puddle of gasoline and into his room.

He cupped one hand over his nose and made his way toward the flames that were shooting up through the smoke. Coughing violently, he tried to get to the sink. With his other hand, he waved away smoke and noticed the source of the fire—a pot on Arnie's hot plate!

Just as Frank felt as if his lungs were going to collapse, he heard a *whooshing* noise. "Wherever you are, Frank—duck!'' It was Joe, with a fire extinguisher.

The chemical stream hit the hot plate and sent it flying off the table, which in turn yanked the plug out of the wall. Joe doused the flames and then spun around to see the doorway behind them blocked by a wall of fire. The puddle of gasoline had just caught.

Joe's fire extinguisher was low. But there was enough to put out the new blaze. Joe shot a steady stream at the doorway as he grabbed Frank and dragged him through the flames and into the hall. He propped his brother near an open window and told him to breathe deeply. Out of the corner of his eye, he saw the fire trucks arriving below.

''Frank! Are you all right?''

Frank's eyes fluttered for a moment and then flicked open. ''I'm okay,'' he said, coughing. He smiled and continued to cough. ''But I'll never understand why people smoke cigarettes. Is that the Kirkland Fire Department I hear?''

''Plus half the school administration—in pajamas! Not to mention all the students in this dorm.''

They heard heavy footsteps climbing the stairs behind them. Joe's wig was lying in the middle of the hallway, and as they looked at it, they realized Joe had to beat it. ''If they catch you here, we'll both be in trouble!'' Frank said.

Joe pushed past a small crowd of kids and disappeared down the far set of stairs.

An overweight fireman came puffing up to the third floor. "You start this fire?" he asked, breathing heavily.

"No," Frank said, rising to his feet. "I just put it out." He walked into his room with the fireman lumbering behind. As they examined the burned pot, the hallway filled up with students, fire fighters, and faculty.

"Can't tell what was in there, Chief," the fireman said, showing the pot to his supervisor. On the bottom were the remains of some badly charred objects.

"You did a good job with the fire extinguisher, young man," the fire chief said to Frank. "Do you have any idea how this all happened? Where are your roommates?"

"One's with his parents in the city. I don't know where the other is, but his car is in the parking lot."

"Well, when he comes back, I wish you'd give him a little talking to. You know, this year alone, over fifty percent of all campus fires—"

The hallway began to clear as Frank listened to a long lecture on fire safety. Out of the corner of his eye, he caught a glimpse of Mr. Castigan, shaking his head disapprovingly.

Frank grabbed some clothes and his copy of *Henry V*, then spent the night on the floor in the room next door. The smell of smoke lingered throughout the night, despite the fact that the fire department had left a giant exhaust fan in the hallway.

The next morning Frank got ready for his study session with Sarah. As he left his neighbors' room, he saw a team of school workers laying a new carpet in the hallway.

"You guys work fast," Frank said.

"That's what you pay Chartwell for!" one of the men answered. Frank looked at the singed doorway, then scanned his room as he wondered where Arnie had spent the night. Wet papers were scattered everywhere, wooden chairs and desks were charred, and large burn marks were on the wall by the hot plate. A film of ashes covered everything.

"The furniture men come this afternoon," the man said. "And the painters'll be here tomorrow."

"Thanks." As Frank walked to Van Cott Hall, he thought about the fire. Obviously someone knew about him and was trying to scare him off. The fire was no mistake—the bucket of gasoline proved that. But the only people who had keys to the room were his roommates and the administration. Did Arnie do it? Did Brad arrange to have it done long-distance?

These questions ran through Frank's mind as he signed into the girls' dorm. He knocked on room 21, and the door was flung open to reveal a gleeful Sarah.

"Congratulations!" she said, gesturing for him to come in. Then she looked at him more closely. "What's the matter? I thought you'd be happy."

"Why?" he asked.

"Didn't they get in touch with you? The administration met late yesterday and decided not to suspend you—just as I said! All they're going to do is keep a close eye on you."

Frank's mood lifted. "That's a relief!" he said. "I was on my phone a lot yesterday afternoon and then I went out early. No one could have told me."

"Oh," said Sarah. Suddenly Frank noticed two other girls staring at them. "I'm sorry," Sarah said. "These are my roommates, Rachel and Alexis. They'll be studying here today, so I figured we'd go out by the river, okay? It's a really nice day."

As they walked to the river, Frank told Sarah about the fire.

"You poor guy," she said, spreading a blanket under a maple tree by the river. "Will you be awake enough to study?"

"Sarah, the image of Mr. Osborn handing me a paper marked *F* makes me very alert."

Sarah and Frank talked about *Henry V* for two solid hours before they rested. Frank was beginning to feel slightly better about the test. He sat up and leaned back against the tree, looking out at the crew rowing on the river.

Sarah leaned back, too, so that her shoulder brushed against Frank's.

"Oops! Sorry!" Frank said.

"No, keep it there. This is comfortable." Two bright orange leaves twisted to the ground in front of them. Sarah smiled at Frank.

"I think I'll close my eyes and wish I were floating down the river," she said. "Past tropical jungles and forests—" She leaned her head against Frank's right shoulder.

Frank immediately thought about Callie. Somehow, though, she seemed very far away. He didn't know if it was the autumn air, or the relief he felt about the test, or Sarah's smile—but he felt very happy to be there with her.

"You know, Sarah, you make Shakespeare seem easy," he said.

"Mmm." She smiled. "By the way, I brought us some things for us to eat. They're in my backpack."

"I'll get it," Frank said, reaching to his left.

"No, let me!" Sarah said insistently. Frank sat back and Sarah reached across him, and the two of them came face-to-face. For a long moment they both forgot about the backpack, and slowly their lips drew closer.

"Hey! What is this? Some kind of soap opera?"

Frank and Sarah pulled away from each other.

Looming above them, dressed in crew clothes, was another of the "jurors" from Frank's tribunal—Stu Goldman.

His face was twisted with jealous rage. And clenched in his hand was an eight-foot wooden oar.

Chapter

9

"STU! WHAT ARE you doing here?" Sarah exclaimed.

"Crew practice! What does it look like?" said Stu.

"Hello, Stu," said Frank. "We were just discussing *Henry the Fifth*. Would you like to join—"

"Don't be flip with me, new boy!" Stu said. He kicked Frank's book aside. "You're having a lot of fun breaking rules and getting away with it—but you're not going to break rule number one!"

"What's rule number one?" asked Frank.

Stu imitated Frank's voice: " 'What's rule number one?' It's simple, Kenyon. Thou shalt not steal someone else's girlfriend!"

Frank shot a surprised look at Sarah.

"No, Stu, you know it's over," said Sarah evenly. "I'm tired of you thinking you own me—"

"Please leave, Sarah," Stu growled. "This is between him and me!"

"Stu—"

"Sarah, *please leave!*" Stu was shouting now.

"Come on, Stu," Frank said. "Leave her alone."

"What are you, her protector?" Stu asked, giving Frank a nudge in the ribs with his oar. "Her Romeo?" Frank got up and backed away; Stu poked him again. "Her knight in shining armor?" Another poke.

"Knock it off, Stu," Frank said, barely containing his anger.

"I'll knock *you* off," Stu said. This time he jabbed Frank in the stomach, knocking the wind out of him.

That did it. Frank picked up a thick branch and held it out in front of him.

While Sarah looked on in horror, visions of what Stu could do with the oar flashed through Frank's head. At least this guy is normal sized, he thought. If I can beat that oar—

Stu's eyes flashed wildly. "Oh, you want to fight, do you?" He tried to ram Frank with the oar, but Frank hopped out of the way. Stu went flying by him, off balance, and Frank pushed him to the ground with the branch.

Red-faced, Stu clenched his teeth, stood, and

lunged with the oar again. Frank blocked it with the branch. Then Stu charged once again. Frank held his ground.

Clunk! The two weapons made contact and the boys held them steady. "You don't think that twig is going to hold out against this oar, do you?" said Stu as Frank's branch started to crack from the pressure of the stronger oar.

Stu backed Frank to the edge of the river. Frank began to slip in the mud. Stu pushed harder. *Crrrrick!* Frank's branch was not going to make it.

All of a sudden there was a loud crack. Just as Frank's branch split in two, he ducked down. From the force of his pushing, Stu fell forward, tumbled over Frank, and went splashing into the river.

"Stu!" yelled Sarah with concern.

Frank brushed himself off. A crowd of Stu's team members had gathered on the shore to watch. Now they were laughing at Stu.

Stu stood up in the water. He was furious. He climbed out of the river, picked up his oar, raised it high over his head, and ran toward Frank, screaming.

"AAAAAAAGGGHHH!" It was like a war cry. Totally defenseless, Frank ran toward the boathouse. Just as Stu came within striking range, Frank ducked behind a white wooden fence.

Stu swung hard. The oar crashed down onto

the top of the fence. In one swift motion, Frank jumped up and jerked his end of the oar down. Like a seesaw, the other end swung up—and clipped Stu squarely in the jaw. Stunned, he tumbled to the ground and lay there motionless.

Sarah ran over to Stu and cradled his head. Blood trickled from his mouth. Frank knelt down next to her.

"Is he going to be all right?" Sarah asked anxiously.

"He'll come to in a minute." Frank examined Stu's jaw. "At least I didn't knock out any teeth! Boy, my record here is just getting better and better!" He struck his clenched fist against the ground in frustration.

Mr. Harrison, the crew coach, came jogging up to join them. "Give him some room!" he said. "I saw your fight from my boat out on the river. It looked as if he provoked you with one of the oars."

"I'm afraid you're right, Coach Harrison," Sarah said.

By now Stu was beginning to stir. He rubbed his jaw and moaned.

"I'll take care of him," Harrison said. "But then he's going to have to answer a few questions!"

As Coach Harrison helped Stu into the boathouse, Frank and Sarah walked to the dorms.

"How long did you two go out?" Frank asked.

"Two years," Sarah said with a sigh.

"Not that I mind, of course," Frank added quickly. "You see—" He felt he had to say something about Callie but stopped short. He couldn't bring himself to do it.

"What, Frank?"

"I—I just don't picture you two together."

Sarah thought about that for a moment, then threw her arms around Frank and gave him a quick kiss. "Good luck on the test Monday!" With that, she jogged away toward Van Cott Hall.

Frank felt as if he had been hit by a truck. He didn't know if it was because of Stu—or his feelings for Sarah.

By the time he got to the third floor of Mansfield Hall, his mind was back on the investigation. There was a new carpet in the hall and his door had been replaced. But inside, his room was still a mess.

He opened the door to see Arnie, clicking away at a new computer. The char marks on the wall were now covered with pieces of tractor-feed paper that had ugly computer drawings on them.

"Quite a disaster, huh?" Frank said.

Arnie jumped in his seat when he heard Frank's voice. He swung his head around.

"Oh, it's you," he said, turning back to his computer. "You startled me."

"Were you able to salvage your hot plate?" Frank asked.

"Mm-hm."

"Any messages?"

"On the table." Arnie didn't even stop clicking away at his keyboard. Frank looked at the scrawled message. It was from Mr. Castigan, confirming that the board had decided not to expel Frank.

"Hey, Arnie, great news, huh?" Frank said.

"Yeah. Congratulations."

Arnie didn't seem to want to talk. Frank straightened up the room a bit and noticed how many of his things were damaged. He started making a list of the things he would need to replace.

"Can I get you anything at the store?" he asked.

"No." Arnie's voice was tense, almost hostile.

His stupid pot almost destroyed our room, Frank thought. Why is he acting like this? He remained patient—until Arnie said, without looking up from the computer, "Would you *please* shut the door after you come in? Can't you feel the draft?"

Frank had had enough. He spun Arnie around in his chair and grabbed him by the shoulders. "Look. If you're so concerned about keeping the door closed, then tell me what happened last night! You sure didn't remember to shut it behind you *after you started that fire!*"

Arnie looked as if his eyes would pop out of his head. He shook as he answered Frank, and the words gushed out of him: "You're just like Brad! He won't leave me alone! He thinks I did

72

it, too. You guys hate me! *I* didn't set the fire—I couldn't have even if I'd wanted to. I lost my keys when I was out, and I couldn't find anyone to let me in. I thought *you* set the fire!"

Frank let go of him and Arnie sank back into his seat. "Why don't you just leave me alone, okay?" Arnie said softly. "My computer was completely destroyed. I had to get my father to wire me money to rent this one."

"Sorry, Arnie," said Frank. "Did you find your keys?"

"No, I camped out in a friend's room till I heard about the fire. Then the maintenance men gave me keys to the new lock this afternoon. Yours are on your bed."

"Listen, Arnie, maybe you can help me find out who set the fire. Where did you lose your keys last night?"

"At the Young Turk. It's a hangout that all the kids in the area go to, in Kirkland."

"Were there any other Chartwell students there?"

"A few, but nobody I knew—"

"Nobody?" Frank asked.

"Well, except one. But he's there practically every night."

"Who's that, Arnie?"

"That jerk Dwight Trilby."

Chapter

10

"So how's the old gut? Want some leftover fish?" Brad slapped Frank on the back as he barged into the room early that evening.

"What?" Frank was puzzled for a moment.

Brad put on a TV newscaster's voice: "Frank Kenyon, the latest victim of 'Rogers's Revenge'! Story at eleven."

"Oh!" Frank remembered—Mr. Rogers lied to Brad about why Frank had left dinner early. "Wow, did I feel terrible after that meal! Sorry I cut out."

"Hey, no problem, buddy. The old man was pretty shaken up about it, though. After you split, he got cranky and left the table early to work on his computer."

Frank's ears perked up. "Really? What does

74

he need to do on his computer on a Friday night?"

"Some bank stuff. I don't know, it's all Greek to me."

I wonder if he's lying, Frank thought.

"Want to play a little tennis?" Brad asked.

"Not now," said Frank. "I have to study for this English exam. And so do you!"

"But it's a Saturday night! Besides, I saw the movie of *Henry the Fifth* this summer. I'll fudge my way through the exam. See you later!" Brad grabbed his racket and left.

Frank went back to work. He studied the rest of the night and all day Sunday. He was determined to hold his own against his classmates on the test, especially now that he'd been given a second chance at Chartwell.

The night before the exam he tossed and turned with horrible dreams. In one dream, the exam was thirty pages long. It was written in a language he didn't understand. Everyone else finished it in ten minutes, but it took Frank three days. When he finally handed it in, Mr. Osborn took one look at it and burst out laughing. Osborn ran out to show it to Mr. Castigan, who became furious. Castigan decided to call up Frank personally and expel him. Frank's phone rang—and rang—

"Wake up, Frank! It's for you!"

"No. No! I won't! Wh-what?" Frank opened his eyes and saw Arnie handing him a phone.

"Take this," Arnie said. "I'm running late for class!"

He scooted out the door as Frank grabbed the phone and shouted, "Mr. Castigan, please! Let me take the exam again! Just one more chance—"

"You have had enough chances, young man!" said the voice on the other end. Then there was silence, followed by loud laughter. "Frank, it's me, Joe! Calm down! You having nightmares or something?"

Frank realized where he was and what had happened. "Oh. Sorry. You're right!"

"Can you talk? Any progress on Wilson?"

Frank looked around. He was alone in the room. "Nothing," he said. "But I have a new lead on Dwight Trilby."

"Mr. Trilby's son? You think *he* did it?"

Frank's eyes widened when he looked at his alarm clock. He had overslept. "Joe, I can't talk now. Meet me tonight, eight o'clock, at the Young Turk, Kirkland, and I'll tell you about it, so you can report to Dad. I've got a big day with this English exam!"

"What? You know, you are becoming an absolute nerd, Frank!"

"Listen. It's bad enough *you* were kicked out of here. If I flunk out, we'll never get to the bottom of this case!" Frank said.

The school day seemed to drag on forever until English period. As Frank walked to class, he felt nervous. He entered and took his usual seat next to Brad.

"If it isn't the great scholar!" said Brad. "Good luck."

"Thanks, Brad." At the sound of Frank's voice, Sarah turned around and smiled warmly at Frank, giving him a wink.

Brad saw this and nudged Frank in the ribs. "Not bad, Kenyon," he said. "But very brave! Very brave—"

Frank guessed Brad was talking about Stu, but he'd have to ask Brad later. Mr. Osborn was handing out the exams.

It wasn't as bad as his dream. In fact, Frank found that he could answer just about all of the questions. He even remembered lines from the play. The hour flew by, and Frank finished just in time.

After it was over, he met Sarah in the hallway. "How was it?" she asked.

"Easier than I expected, thanks to you," Frank said. They walked down the hallway, talking about their answers. By the time they stopped in front of Frank's next class, he felt relieved.

"Sounds like we had just about the same answers," said Sarah.

"That either means I did very well, or some of my ignorance rubbed off on you," Frank answered.

"Well, I think you should be proud of yourself

and relax the rest of the day," Sarah said. She grabbed his hand, squeezed it, and walked off.

Frank was about to go into his social studies class when he heard a loud kissing sound.

"Oh, Frank, sweetheart, come read me Shakespeare tonight!" It was Brad, imitating a female voice.

"Knock it off, Brad," Frank said.

"Are you moving in on Sarah?" Brad asked. "I thought she and Stu were getting back together again."

"Not according to Sarah," Frank said.

"You should've told me that earlier. I could have reminded them when I saw them holding hands behind the tennis courts yesterday! Hate to spoil your fun, buddy—but be careful." With that, he walked off to his next class.

Well, that's really none of my business, thought Frank. But somehow, as he walked to his class, he couldn't help but feel a little uneasy about what Brad had told him.

As Frank approached the Young Turk that night, dozens of students were hanging around outside. Some had blazers or skirts with Chartwell or Winchester embroidered on them. But there was no sign of Dwight Trilby.

At the front door, Frank was met by a familiar-looking student.

"That'll be one dollar," he said. As Frank

reached into his pocket, the guy said, "Frank Kenyon, right?"

"Yes, and you're—"

"Ty Farnsworth, I was on the student tribunal, remember?" he said, smiling. "My father owns this place. I work the front door whenever he can't get anyone."

Frank handed him a dollar. "Skip it," whispered Ty. "To make up for the tribunal. Between you and me, I'm glad they didn't take our recommendation. You didn't deserve to be expelled."

"Thanks, Ty." Frank peered past Ty into the club. There, arm wrestling at a table near the window, was Dwight Trilby. "By the way," Frank said to Ty, "were you here Friday night?"

"Yes."

"I hear Dwight Trilby was in good form that night."

Ty laughed. "Just the usual. You know, picking fights with guys, trying to show off for the sophomore girls—"

"Was he here the whole night?"

"I don't know. Oh, yeah, I do remember him leaving for a while and then coming back."

Frank smiled. "What a party animal. Oh, I almost forgot—did anyone return a set of keys to you that night?"

Ty thought for a second, then shook his head. "No, definitely not. Lots of questions, huh?"

Frank smiled and went into the club to look

around. Dwight Trilby was the only person he recognized, but Frank kept his distance. The last thing he wanted was a repeat of Wednesday's party.

At eight o'clock Frank stepped outside. He saw Joe standing by the Hardy van. He trotted over to him.

"What is this club?" Joe asked.

"For future white-collar criminals," Frank said. "Dwight Trilby is a regular here. He was in the place the night my roommate Arnie lost his keys. *And* he left here and came back at one point during the night."

"That's great, Frank, but somehow I don't think it'll hold up in court."

"Well, it's a start. The guy is a real slime ball, and I think we should keep an eye on him. See if you can dig up anything from your end—talk to Mr. Trilby, check into Dwight's accounts."

"Will do!" said Joe. "Want a lift back to campus?"

"I'll drive," said Frank, hopping into the driver's seat.

"Hey, wait a min—" Joe said, starting to protest.

"Come on, you've been using it all week. Anyway, you drive like a stockcar racer." Frank started up the van. "Now get in. I'll drive us to the back entrance of Mansfield Hall. We don't want any of the wrong people seeing you. Then you can take the van home with you."

"I'm touched by your generosity," Joe said. "By the way, how'd the exam go this afternoon?"

"At least a B plus," said Frank with a grin. *"I'm* a pretty good test taker."

Frank drove into campus. As he pulled quietly around Mansfield Hall, Joe said, "I think you ought to do some legwork on this Wilson character. He—"

"Shhhh!" Frank said. "What's going on here?" In front of them was an old foreign sports car. A familiar-looking student was walking from the car to the dorm, with an armload of boxes. When he saw Frank and Joe's van, he froze.

"Jed?" Frank called. "Is that you?"

At that, Jed threw his boxes back into the car, jumped into the front seat, and tore away into the night.

"Hey! That's the kid that guy Barry was beating up for laughing about his radio! *That's* Jed Wilson? What's he up to?" Joe asked.

"Buckle your seat belt," Frank said to Joe. "We're about to find out."

The van's tires squealed as Frank gunned the accelerator.

"Step on it, Frank! He's got a big head start!"

Frank and Joe sped through the campus after Jed. Frank flicked on his brights. He saw Jed's car screeching around the administration building toward the front gate.

"Hang on!" Frank shouted. He drove toward the building at top speed. The van lurched to the right as he swung left around the building. Cutting across the lawn, Frank headed straight for the gate.

But by this time, Jed was outside on the road, past the gate. He had stopped his car and hopped out. As the van raced toward him, Jed grabbed the gate and swung it closed.

"Look out, Frank! That's wrought iron!" Joe yelled.

"I can't stop!" Frank shouted back.

Chapter

11

FRANK PRESSED ON the brakes. The van skidded to one side, then the other. Frank realized they were going to crash. In a split second, he yanked the steering wheel sharply to the right. The van veered away from the gate and onto the lawn. It ripped across the grass, straight toward a tall hedge.

"Where are we going?" asked Joe in a panic.

"He took the high road, and we'll take the low!" said Frank. The van crashed through hedge and onto a side street.

"Much easier on the grillwork," said Frank as he drove toward the main road. "Now, which way did he go?"

"Toward Kirkland, I think!" Joe said. The air filled with the smell of burning rubber as Frank stepped on the gas.

They careened around a bend in the road. Frank eased up on the pedal. Then he moved his foot to gun the accelerator again—until he saw that he was about fifty feet from a line of cars stopped at a light.

"Stop! Stop!" Joe screamed. Frank hit the brake and the brothers jerked forward. The van's tires left long, black lines as it headed straight for the last car.

"Detour!" Frank said. He steered the van onto the shoulder of the road, where it came to a stop in the tall grass.

"Hey, where'd you get your license—a department store?" one driver shouted back at them.

The light ahead of the cars had turned green. Slowly the long line began to snake forward.

"Look," said Joe. "There's Wilson, third from the back. Now we've got him."

As if on cue, Jed's car pulled out of the line and onto the shoulder in front of Frank and Joe.

Frank stepped on the accelerator—but the van wouldn't move.

"We're stuck. The wheels are spinning!"

"I'll push!" Joe replied. He hopped out of the van and braced himself against the back.

After the second heave, the van edged out of the rut. Joe hopped in and they took off.

The ride along the bumpy shoulder jostled the brothers. Far ahead of them, they could see Jed moving back onto the street.

Frank pulled back on the road, right behind a

silver-haired man in a dark green Porsche. "Come on, move it!" shouted Joe as he reached over and pressed the van's horn.

"There's an easier way than that," said Frank. Before them, the road stretched out into a straightaway. Frank pulled into the left lane to pass the car. As he sped past, he glanced over at the man in the sports car.

It was Mr. Rogers.

"The plot thickens," Frank said. He floored the gas pedal and took off in a burst of speed. After he pulled in front, he checked the rearview mirror. The sports car had speeded up and was now gaining on them.

"Don't look now, but we've gone from being the chaser to the chasee," said Frank. He suddenly made a sharp left onto a side street. Joe's right shoulder banged into the door as the tires screamed.

"Ouch!" Joe yelled.

"Sorry about that," said Frank. He saw Rogers's car in the rearview mirror as he swung right at the next block. Quickly he turned left, left, and right among the residential streets of Kirkland. The small side streets were pretty much deserted. Only one old brick building they passed was well lit up. Frank barreled on by it.

All of a sudden the night air was pierced by a siren.

"That was the police station, Frank!" Joe cried, slapping his forehead.

A squad car pulled out of the station with its lights glaring. Frank pulled the van over to the curb. The car stopped behind him, and a police officer got out and slowly walked to the van.

"I'm glad I let *you* drive," Joe said sarcastically.

The officer looked into the van. "Testing out the streets, boys?" he said. "They work all right for you?"

"Sorry, officer, I got carried away," Frank answered.

"Maybe we can discuss this in the station house. You can leave your van here, and let it catch its breath."

Frank and Joe followed the officer into the station house down the block. As they crossed the street, Mr. Rogers drove slowly by them, staring at Frank.

The officer brought Frank and Joe into a drab but brightly lit room with five molded plastic chairs. "Have a seat, gentlemen," he said. "And I'll take your license and registration, please."

While writing out the summons, the officer walked slowly back and forth. It seemed like hours before he finished.

"Okay, Mr. Hardy," he said to Frank. "All I'm allowed to do is give you a speeding ticket. But I have a message for you—next time you pass through Kirkland, you better be extra careful, because I can make life very rough for you. Understood?"

Frank nodded and took his ticket. The officer said, "Now I want you to give the keys to your friend here, who will drive you and your van very slowly out of town."

Joe took the keys, trying to hold back a grin, and the brothers walked back out to the van.

"So," said Joe as they climbed into the van, "you sure you feel safe with a 'stockcar racer' behind the wheel?"

"Score one for you," said Frank. "Now let's get out of here."

"Yes, sir," answered Joe. "And while I'm driving safely, you can tell me why that silver-haired guy was following us."

Frank explained about Rogers as Joe pulled away from the station house.

Joe drove carefully back toward Chartwell, going twenty-five miles an hour, stopping at yellow lights—and generally driving Frank crazy.

"You're doing this on purpose, Joe—" Frank said as Joe slowed to fifteen miles an hour along the road by the river.

"Shhh!" Joe said, interrupting. "What's going on over there?" They both heard a loud splashing noise by the boathouse. As they got closer, they could see the gleam of metal behind a hedge. Joe turned off the headlights and pulled over to the side of the road.

They stepped out of the van and ran quietly across the street to the boathouse. By now they could see that the shining metal was a car, reflecting the light of a street lamp. Beyond it they could make out the silhouette of a person throwing a box into the river.

They sneaked up to the car and immediately recognized it.

"It's Jed's," whispered Frank. He looked inside to see a stack of cardboard boxes in the backseat.

"Why is he trying to get rid of these boxes?" Joe asked. He stuck his head above the car to watch as Jed threw another box into the river. Then Jed turned to walk back to the car.

"Oops," Joe said, ducking down. But it was too late. Jed stopped in his tracks. He looked left and right and then darted onto the dock and into an open side entrance of the darkened boathouse.

Joe immediately ran after him. "Forget it," Frank called out. "You'll never find him in there. Besides, he has to come back to the car eventually."

They opened the car door. The ceiling light shone on the boxes in the backseat. Joe reached in and ripped one open. Inside were a dozen pocket-size devices that looked like electronic beepers. On the side of each was a metal button.

"What in the name of—" Joe picked one up and shook it. He pressed the button and put it up to his ear. No sound.

"Let me try something," Frank said. He took the device and pressed the button, pointing it at the car's ceiling light.

Dzzzzit! With a sputtering sound, the light flickered out.

"I thought that might happen! You know what this is?" said Frank, his eyes glowing with recognition.

Before Joe could answer, both of them were distracted by the sound of squealing brakes. Across the street, a sports car had stopped behind the van. A dark green Porsche.

The door flew open, and Mr. Rogers stepped out. In the glow from the overhead light it was impossible to misread the expression on his face. He oozed anger. He slammed the door and stormed over to Frank and Joe's van and yanked the door open. Seeing nothing, he spun around and walked toward the river. "All right, Kenyon, I know you and your greasy buddy are around somewhere!"

"Greasy?" said Joe. "Hey, where does he get off—"

"Shhh!"

Rogers jerked his head in Frank and Joe's direction. He reached into his breast pocket. Frank's body tensed as he watched Rogers pull out a shiny object.

"It's a gun!" he whispered.

Chapter

12

"QUICK, OUT OF sight!" Frank said. Crouching low, he and Joe ran for the dock of the boathouse and crawled underneath it.

A shot rang out as Rogers ran toward the boathouse. Frank and Joe heard a splash as the bullet sailed over the dock and into the water. Rogers cursed under his breath. The sound of muffled footsteps was all the brothers could hear for the next minute—and then there was total silence.

Carefully, they positioned themselves so they could see out from under the dock.

Rogers had found Jed's car and was examining the contents of the cardboard box.

"He put his pistol away," whispered Frank.

"Maybe he thinks those little electronic things are ray guns or something," said Joe.

From within the boathouse came a crashing noise. Rogers ran toward it, jumped onto the dock, and found the open door.

"Feeling a little clumsy tonight, Kenyon?" he snarled. Pulling a flashlight out of his pocket, he stepped inside.

Dzzzzit! The flashlight flickered out.

"These cheap dime-store pieces of trash!" he muttered to himself. He gave one last look into the boathouse, but obviously could make out nothing in the pitch blackness.

Frank and Joe heard the *crick, crick, crick* of the dock's wooden planks as Rogers walked directly above them.

Then, with a sigh of disgust, Rogers put the flashlight and the electronic device into his pocket and strode back to his car.

As the car drove off, Frank and Joe climbed out from under the dock. "Jed short-circuited Rogers's flashlight, didn't he?" Joe said.

"Right. He must have one of those little gadgets with him," answered Frank.

Joe's voice was filled with excitement. "And those must be the things that—"

He was interrupted by another loud crash from inside the boathouse. Frank and Joe turned toward the sound. A light went on inside. And out from the open door ran Jed Wilson, his face strained with fear.

When he saw Frank and Joe, he turned and ran off the other side of the dock and along the river.

Frank and Joe sprinted after him. In seconds Joe was right behind Jed. He dove through the air and grabbed Jed by the waist, pulling him to the ground in a perfect tackle. From out of Jed's pocket, one of the little devices fell to the ground.

Frank ran up next to them and stood over Jed. He grabbed the device and showed it to Joe. "All right, Wilson," he said. "Something's fishy around here, and I'm not talking only about the boxes you threw in the river. Want to talk?"

Jed's face was taut with anguish. "Okay, okay, I give up!" he blurted out. "Turn me in! I deserve it! Honestly, I didn't mean any harm—"

"Whoa! Slow down," said Joe. "Maybe you should start at the beginning."

"I should have known the minute I invented Electrojam I'd get into trouble. It was just for fun! I didn't realize that everyone would start short-circuiting other people's radios, TV sets, stereos—"

"You mean those little gizmos—Electrojams—are what's blowing out all those box radios?" asked Joe.

"Yes! I admit it," Jed said. "I invented them by mistake, but when I saw what they could do, I decided to sell a few of them through my company, Chip-Shape.

"Usually I just sell software and computer games, but I thought I'd branch out with Electrojam. I thought it could be used for emergency shut-off switches, disarming electronic weapons.

And—once in a while—for sabotaging radios. But I never thought it would get out of hand like that!"

"Could they jam a computer?" Frank asked. Jed nodded. And Frank looked at his brother and smiled. A tie-in.

"Finally, I went to all of my customers and told them I was recalling the Electrojams for a defective part. But really I was planning to destroy them all!"

"Why did you run away from us?" Joe asked.

"Well, I recognized Frank when he came here. And I thought it was only a matter of time before he figured out who I was and what my connection was to the sabotaged radios. When I saw you two tonight, I could tell you were coming after me to turn me in to the school authorities. So I figured the river was the quickest place to dump my Electrojammers. You have to understand how much it means to my parents that I'm at Chartwell—"

"We're not going to turn you in," Frank said.

"You're not?" Jed looked relieved, but puzzled. "Then why are you chasing me?"

Frank thought quickly. "To protect you from the man we just saw. He's my roommate's father, and he works for the Bayport Bank and Trust. I overheard him say that he wanted to trail you."

Joe was getting the idea. "Seems he suspects something about a large withdrawal from your account."

Jed thought for a minute and then nodded his head. "Yes, there was something funny on my last statement. It showed that twenty-five thousand dollars was put in and taken out on the same day. I just thought it was a bank error." He smiled. "I *wish* my company did that much business in a day."

"You have no idea where the money could have gone?" Joe asked.

"Believe me," Jed said. "If I'd had that much, I'd have held on to it!"

Frank and Joe looked at each other. Jed seemed sincere. Could he have been framed?

"Hey-y-y, wait a minute," Jed said, picking himself up from the ground. "You guys are after that money, aren't you?"

"What?" asked Joe. He and Frank exchanged baffled looks.

"Yeah, *you* want to track down a quick twenty-five thousand dollars," he said. "What are you going to do if you can't, steal my idea? Try to get a patent? Oh, I've got your number—"

"Easy, Jed," Frank said. He and Joe hadn't expected that. "You've got this wrong—"

"Prove it," Jed answered, "I dare you."

"We're out of here," Joe muttered to Frank. "Uh, listen, Jed," he said, backing away. "We've enjoyed meeting you, but we can't stay and talk. Maybe some other time—"

With that, Frank and Joe turned to jog back to

the van. "Dad's going to laugh when I tell him about this one," Joe muttered as they climbed in.

Jed stood by the river, hurling insults at them as they drove away.

The next day Frank mulled over the scene with Jed on his way to English class. He was so lost in thought that he walked right by Sarah.

"Hey, why the cold shoulder?" she asked.

"Oh, sorry, Sarah," said Frank. "Guess I'm just tense about getting my exam back today. I still think I blew it."

Sarah laughed. "Something tells me you're in for a surprise," she said.

They sat down in class, and immediately Mr. Osborn started handing out the papers.

"Not bad, most of you," he said as he got to Brad's desk. Out of the corner of his eye, Frank could see Brad's grade: C+. Brad seemed pleased.

"Mr. Pierce—" Osborn continued, "Miss Waterbury—" He handed Sarah her paper. A bright red A− was written at the top. Frank breathed a sigh of relief, realizing his must be close to the same grade.

Sarah turned around and gave Frank a thumbs-up sign. Frank smiled back. Before long Mr. Osborn called out Frank's name and handed over his exam. Frank snatched it eagerly and looked at it. His face fell when he saw the grade.

D−.

He couldn't understand how it happened. He knew his answers were the same as Sarah's. Bewildered, he glanced through the exam. It was full of red marks. He read what he had written—and suddenly it all became clear.

All the answers were different from the ones he remembered, and the handwriting wasn't quite right. Someone had forged his exam and switched it with the real one.

At the end of the exam was a note: "Frank, I expected more from you. Dean Castigan has asked that you see him in his office at the end of the school day—Mr. Osborn."

After class, Frank went up to Mr. Osborn. "I didn't write these answers, Mr. Osborn," he said. "I think someone is playing a trick. This looks like my handwriting, but I swear it's not! Someone substituted this test for mine. Please let me take the exam over."

Mr. Osborn looked at Frank and said, "We might be able to work something out, Frank, but the test has to count. And I'd be careful about making a serious charge like forgery. You're obviously very upset, but I can't do much about it."

Frank stormed into the hallway, where Sarah was waiting. "What happened?" she asked.

"Someone wants me out of Chartwell," Frank said angrily. "And I don't know who."

The rest of the day, he couldn't concentrate in his classes. At the end of last period, he marched down to Mr. Castigan's office.

"Have a seat," Mr. Castigan said gravely. "I need to have a talk with you. You know, you haven't exactly gotten off to a good start at Chartwell."

"Mr. Castigan, my English exam was forged. None of the answers matched the ones I put on the exam. And the handwriting wasn't mine."

Castigan began pacing the floor. "Frank, I have your file here. Let's look at your admissions essay." He pulled out a piece of paper from Frank's admissions file, which was on his desk. Next to it he held up the English exam. "It looks like the same handwriting to me."

"I know. It's a very good forgery. But you've got to believe me!"

"I wish I could, Frank. But I can't ignore what I've seen this week. First it was the episode in the file room, and then the fire in your dorm room. I told the administration not to suspend you, just to keep a close eye on you—because I thought you had potential. But now even your schoolwork is suffering."

"I swear to you, Mr. Castigan—"

"Swearing won't be necessary," Castigan said. He looked directly into Frank's eyes, scowling.

"Claiming forgery is the oldest trick in the book, Frank. You know, students *have* been expelled from Chartwell before. Don't make it worse for yourself. You are definitely on thin ice."

Chapter

13

WHEN HE GOT back to his room at four, Frank pored over his notes on the case. Nothing seemed to fit, and he was having a difficult time concentrating. He wished he could be at home, his feet up in Dad's den, thinking things through. At Chartwell he was never completely free. Arnie was at a math club meeting, and Brad was at the gym, but any minute one of them could come back.

Frank felt angry. Someone was outwitting him. He paced back and forth, wondering who could have forged his writing and switched the exams without Mr. Osborn finding out.

His thoughts were interrupted by a knock at the door. "Who is it?" he asked.

"It's me, Sarah. Can I come in?"

"Uh, just a minute!" His desk was covered

with papers about the case. He scooped everything up, threw it into a manila folder, and shoved it in a desk drawer. "I'll be right there!" he called out. He slammed the drawer shut and walked over to the door.

"Welcome to the Chartwell pigpen!" he said as he opened the door. Sarah looked around. The walls of the room had just been painted, so all of the furniture had been moved to the center of the room. "We haven't had a chance to straighten it out," said Frank with a shrug.

"Hey, I'm used to this," Sarah said. "I have brothers." She looked closely at Frank. He smiled but kept a cool distance. "Is something wrong, Frank? What took you so long to come to the door? What was that shuffling I heard?"

"Shuffling? I was probably practicing my tap dancing." Frank grinned, hoping she'd drop the subject.

Sarah laughed. "Come on, something's bothering you. Is it the English exam? You never told me what you got on it." She went to sit down on his desk chair, but a piece of paper had fallen onto it. She picked it up and read out loud, " 'Chartwell computer scam—notes re: suspected students and personnel—Frank Hardy.' What does all this mean?"

Frank grabbed the paper from her and pretended to look at it as if he'd never seen it. "Hmm, what's this? Maybe Brad's writing a school newspaper article."

"Under the pen name 'Frank Hardy'?" Sarah gave him a knowing look. "You're trying to pull something, aren't you?"

Frank sat at the edge of his desk. "Sarah, I'm sorry. I can't talk right now about certain things. But someday—"

"Don't you feel you can trust me, Frank? I trust you."

Frank looked straight into her eyes. She looked so open and hurt. He began to feel some of the same things he had felt by the river on Saturday. She was demanding an answer from him. But he realized he, too, had something to settle.

"I'm not sure I do trust you," he said. "Tell me the truth—are you still seeing Stu Goldman? Someone told me he saw you two behind the tennis courts the other day."

Sarah's face turned red. "It must have been that snob roommate of yours, Brad Rogers. I saw him giving us a look." She shook her head and smiled sadly.

"Poor Stu. He was following me around like a puppy dog, trying to apologize for that fight with you. I had to talk to him for about two hours when he cornered me behind the courts, but I laid it on the line, and he finally took no for an answer."

Frank nodded. "I see—"

"Okay. You have my story. Now you owe me one."

Frank hung his head. He didn't know what to

do. The mission had to be a secret; Frank and Joe had both agreed to that. But Sarah was so trusting—and besides, she was one of the brightest people he had met. Maybe she would be a help in cracking the case. Anyway, she already knew too much, after seeing that piece of paper. It would be better to try to get her on his side. He took one more look into her questioning blue eyes and decided what to do. He took a deep breath, hoping he was doing the right thing.

"Will you promise me two things, Sarah?" he asked.

"Name them."

"Don't think I'm crazy, keep this whole thing secret, and promise to help me out."

Sarah grinned slyly. "That's three promises. Do I get to choose which two to keep?"

"Picky, picky," Frank said. He explained the whole story to her. She listened with wide-eyed amazement.

"So what happens now?" she asked when he finished talking.

Frank paced the room again. "Well, just before you got here I was thinking. Now the thief is obviously using a computer to transfer the money. He must have intimate knowledge of the Bayport Bank and Trust. And he must also have a modem, which he uses to send signals through the phone to the bank computer—"

"And," Sarah said, cutting in, "if you find out

which students have modems, you narrow the field!"

"I can tell already that you're detective material!" Frank said. "Now, from what I've researched, there's only one computer store in Kirkland. For starters, I can find out how many modems have been sold to Chartwell students from there."

"The trick will be getting the store owner to cooperate with you," said Sarah.

"Which is where a famous detective father comes in handy." Frank picked up the phone and dialed his father's number. For once, Fenton Hardy was there.

"Hello? Dad, it's Frank. . . . Well, I'm trying a new tactic. Can you meet me in an hour at a store called Campus Computer in Kirkland? . . . Good! . . . See you there!"

Frank hung up the phone and slapped his palms together. "He says he'll drive right there and explain everything to the proprietor. I'd better get ready."

Sarah put her hands on her hips. "You don't plan on going *alone,* do you?"

"You want to come?"

Sarah nodded enthusiastically.

Frank smiled. "Why not? You're involved already!"

Together they took the long walk into Kirkland. The air had become brisk, and it whipped against them as they passed by open fields. Sarah snuggled up against Frank. She looked up at him with sparkling eyes. "Did anyone ever tell you that from a certain angle you look like"—she searched for a name—"you know, what's his name?"

"The guy who played Superman in the movies?"

"Yeah! How did you know that's what I was thinking?"

Frank blushed. He wished Joe had been here to hear that.

When they reached Main Street, Frank saw Fenton's car parked in front of a small store. Bolted into the gray, wooden shingles above the front door was the Campus Computer sign. Frank and Sarah walked inside and saw Fenton talking to the store owner.

"Ah, Mr. Dodd," said Fenton. "This is my son Frank and—"

"Sarah Waterbury. This is my dad, Fenton Hardy," said Frank. "She's a friend from school. She knows everything."

Frank could sense his father wasn't happy he had told Sarah about the mission, but Fenton's attention was soon drawn back to Mr. Dodd.

"I'd be glad to show you my modem sales, Mr. Hardy," he said. "But I might as well save you the trouble. You see, Chartwell Academy does not allow its students to own modems. They tried it last year, but found there was too much cheating. Students there are very competitive, and they were finding creative ways to steal each other's work.''

Frank felt deflated. "You mean there are no modems at all at Chartwell?"

"None that are legal—and certainly none that were bought here by students.''

"What about nonstudents?" said Fenton. "You know, faculty, administration—"

"Come to think of it," Mr. Dodd replied, flipping through his list, "I *did* sell one to the—uh—ah, here it is! The admissions office!"

Frank, Fenton, and Sarah thanked Mr. Dodd and left the store. "Not much of a help, is it?" said Sarah.

"Unless there's some crooked admissions official," answered Frank.

"Can you get into the admissions office?" asked Fenton.

"I've done it before and botched it," Frank said. "But it looks like I'm going to have to try again."

"Come on," said Fenton. "I'll give you kids a ride back."

That night, around ten o'clock, Frank waited in his room until he saw the Hardy van pull around to the back of Mansfield Hall. He rushed out to meet Joe.

Joe hopped out of the van, dressed all in black. "This time there'll be no mistakes," he said.

"There'd better not be," Frank remarked. "Or we can kiss this whole case goodbye."

In the cool autumn night they walked through the empty campus to the administration building. Again, the door was open.

"You'd think they'd have learned their lesson by now," Joe said.

"Maybe they've tried, but someone outsmarted them," Frank said. He pointed to the floor. There, lying near the base of the door, were five bobby pins. Obviously, someone had used them to pick the lock.

"Somebody's in there!" said Joe.

"Brilliant! Now keep it quiet for a while!"

They tiptoed up the stairway to the third floor. The hallway was dark except for a dim light coming from under the admissions office. They crept closer and began to hear a hum.

"It's a computer," said Frank.

"No kidding!"

Just then they heard the scraping of a chair against the floor, and then footsteps.

"Quick! In here!" said Joe, opening up a door beside them. They popped inside and closed the door softly behind them. They were in a small closet. All around them were brooms and mops, and on a shelf above were paper products and cleaning supplies. They heard the footsteps come out into the hallway. Then they became muffled. A water faucet was turned on.

"The bathroom," Joe said. Frank listened as the footsteps became louder again.

"Typical Chartwell bathroom—no paper towels . . ." The voice they heard muttering in the hallway was a male voice, familiar to Frank. The footsteps came closer.

Frank and Joe froze as they heard the doorknob in front of them move. Get ready to run, Joe thought to himself.

But the door didn't open. The voice cursed softly, and the footsteps retreated.

"I don't believe it," whispered Joe. "We're locked in! What a stroke of dumb luck. How long is our air going to last?"

"Shhh," answered Frank. "It's open."

"Then how come he couldn't—"

"Simple. I just held the knob tight. He just *thought* the door was locked." He grinned. "Sometimes the oldest tricks are the best."

Frank pushed open the door slowly. The hallway was empty. The Hardys walked silently along the wall beside the admissions office. They heard the clicking of a computer keyboard. Joe stayed back while Frank carefully looked into the half-open doorway.

There, sitting at the office computer with his back to them, was Dwight Trilby.

Chapter

14

FRANK BACKED AWAY from the door and gestured for Joe to follow. "It's Trilby's son," he whispered.

"Let's get him!" said Joe.

"Not so fast. He's a real moose—six-feet-four. We've got to plan this."

"Why don't we make some noise? As soon as he gets to the door—*wham-mo!* You wrestle him to the ground—and I help!"

"All right," said Frank. He moved closer to the door and took out his key ring. Joe hopped around to the other edge and did the same.

Frank shook his keys gently. They made a soft metallic jingle. He paused and then repeated the motion.

Joe waited for a moment and then began to jingle his keys, too.

As they continued, they could hear that the computer clicking had stopped.

"What the—" said Dwight.

There was silence for a few seconds. Then the clicking started up again.

"Any more bright ideas?" whispered Frank. He and Joe walked away from the door.

"Forget the finesse," said Joe. "Let's just confront him. What's he going to do against two of us?"

As the brothers talked over what to do next, neither of them noticed the sound of a window opening from within the office.

Dwight's voice again broke the stillness. "Hey, who are you?" he asked. Frank and Joe froze. They heard the scraping movement of the chair again. Frank went to the door and looked through the crack.

His mouth dropped open. A man wearing a ski mask had climbed in through the window. In his hand was a gun, pointed straight at Dwight.

Dwight stood up from his chair. The man stepped toward him. Slowly, Dwight put his hands in the air. "You know you're not going to get away with this," he said.

The man answered him with a slam to the stomach. Dwight let out a cry of pain and doubled over. In one swift move, the man reached into his pocket, pulled out a small aerosol spray can, and grabbed Dwight by his hair, forcing his head up.

Then he sent a mist of spray into his victim's face.

"*Now* let's go!" said Joe.

"We can't," answered Frank. "He'll blow our brains out."

The masked man heard their voices. He wheeled around and stepped toward the door, but then decided to back out through the window.

Frank and Joe rushed in. Dwight was leaning helplessly against the wall, coughing. Frank brought the chair over to him and made him sit down. "Can you talk?" Frank said.

"Yeah," Dwight answered in a surly voice. "What do you want? Is *he* one of your stooges?" He indicated the open window with a head movement.

"No," answered Joe. "He doesn't look like anyone we know. Of course, it was hard to tell behind the mask."

"Why don't you begin explaining what you're doing here, Dwight," said Frank. "The administration's not going to look too kindly on this."

"I'll call your bluff," Dwight said. "You're not going to say a thing to anyone. I know all about your little tribunal last week, and the fire in your room. I think *you're* the one who should do the explaining."

"Okay, fair enough," Frank answered. "We're private investigators looking into a scam involving computer transfers of money from your father's bank. And you, my friend, are currently our number-one suspect. What do you have to say to that?"

Dwight looked at Frank in disbelief. Then he started to laugh. "*You're* looking into those thefts? How can I believe you?"

"Your father called us in on the case," said Frank. "He contacted our father, Fenton Hardy, who's a detective. We're Frank and Joe Hardy."

Dwight's eyes suddenly became friendlier. "You're the Hardy brothers! Why didn't you tell me? We could have worked together! I'm trying to get to the bottom of this, too." He looked at Frank. "I've felt so angry about the transfers because no one seemed to be doing anything."

"Is that why you were looking for a fight at the party last week?" Frank asked.

Dwight turned red. "Oh, sorry about that. I get a little hotheaded sometimes—"

"That's okay," said Frank, secretly happy to see Dwight squirm a little. "Tell me, you didn't have anything to do with that fire in my room?"

"No, but I remember your little roommate— Arno, or whatever his name is—looking around for his keys at the Young Turk that same night."

Joe spoke up. "You may be on the level, Trilby, but you still haven't told us what you're doing here."

Dwight pointed over to the computer. "It's obvious someone's been getting at the bank through the computer system. I figured I'd keep track of the bank's records through the computers at Chartwell. My dad doesn't know it, but I made a copy of the bank's system disk."

"So why the admissions office in the middle of the night?" Frank asked.

"Well, I began realizing how many computer nerds there were in this school. One kid even has his own company. And the other night, when I was home for dinner, I overheard my dad saying that this guy's company had gotten a mysterious twenty-five-thousand dollar transfer through the bank's computers. So I decided to check on some student records, to see if I could come up with anything at all that would help me get a lead on this scam." He pointed over to the computer.

"Right now, though, I'm keeping an eye on the bank records." On the screen was a spreadsheet of account numbers and balances. Frank and Joe went to look.

All at once, Dwight whacked Joe on the arm. The brothers whipped around. Dwight was facing them with his fists clenched and his eyes glaring wildly.

"I knew we couldn't trust him," Joe said. Dwight came at them, arms flailing. Frank squared off against him as Joe dove at his feet. Dwight fell to the ground. Joe maneuvered around to lock Dwight in a wrestling hold, but Dwight was too strong. He broke away and stood up. Jumping around in circles, he began striking everything in sight—tables, file cabinets, chairs. Joe went after him.

"Stop, Joe!" Frank called out. "Something's wrong."

"What's he saying?" Joe panted. Dwight was yelling nonsense words now and swinging his arms wildly. His eyes darted rapidly in all directions.

"He's going wild!" said Joe.

"It's that spray the masked guy used on him," Frank said. "He's hallucinating."

"What should we do? He's going to destroy himself and this whole office!"

"Let's try to hold him down before he hurts himself."

They approached Dwight from both sides. But as soon as he noticed them, he let out a scream and ran out the open door.

He bounded down the stairs and out the front door, with Frank and Joe in hot pursuit. With the speed of a sprinter, he ran across campus. Most of the buildings were dark, except for Van Cott Hall, where a party to celebrate no school the next day was in progress. Dwight dashed through the hedge that Frank had flattened in the van the night before. When Frank and Joe got to the street, Dwight was nowhere to be seen.

"You go left and I'll go r—" Frank started to say, but he stopped short when he heard the wild barking of a dog. They ran through a wooded area toward the sound.

In seconds they were in the backyard of a large old house. A black Labrador retriever was snarl-

112

ing at Dwight. Lights in the second-floor windows began to pop on.

Dwight stood stock-still for a moment. Then he saw something in a wood pile near the house. He ran over to it and pulled out an ax.

He lifted the ax above his head and ran toward the dog.

"Dwight! No!" shouted Frank. At the sound of his voice, Dwight spun around and came toward Frank and Joe with the ax.

"Split!" Frank said as Dwight swung the ax at him. The blade came down and embedded itself in a tree.

"I think he took you literally," said Joe. The two of them backed away as Dwight yanked the ax out. With crazed determination, he chased Frank and Joe back into the street. The brothers ran out to the main road.

"Over that ridge!" Joe said. They crossed the road and clambered over a high mound into a meadow.

"Now what?" said Frank.

"Hang tight, we may have lost him." They crawled to the ridge and looked over it. There was no sign of Dwight.

"We lost him, all right," said Frank. "But he can't be left alone. Come on."

They hopped back onto the main road. Frank went through the campus gate and looked around while Joe scanned the nearby woods. After a few minutes they met by the side of the road.

"Nothing," said Joe.

"Let's just hope he's in the woods somewhere, sleeping it off."

At that moment a distant clang of metal rang through the air. Frank and Joe looked around.

"The water tower!" Joe said, pointing in the distance.

Frank looked up. High above them, Dwight was climbing the spiral metal stairs of the Kirkland water tower, dragging the ax behind him.

"He's going to kill himself!" Frank said, and he and Joe ran through the woods toward the tower. They hopped the fence that surrounded it and started climbing the metal stairs, two at a time.

From above them, a stifled scream rang out.

"Don't do anything, Dwight!" Joe called up. "We're here to help you!"

Frank and Joe reached the top of the stairs, a hundred feet above Kirkland, where there was a narrow, curved walkway around the entire water tank. Frank motioned for Joe to go to the left while he went right. Dwight was looking over the railing to the ground below, crying. Lying by his feet was the ax.

"It's okay, Dwight," said Frank, walking slowly toward Dwight with an outstretched hand. The sound of Frank's voice seemed to startle Dwight. He let out a yelp and picked up the ax.

"Stay 'way—back," he mumbled, his eyes

flashing with insane anger. Then he lunged toward Frank, swinging the ax.

Frank ducked away. The ax clanked loudly against the side of the water tank. This made Dwight become even more furious. He took small steps toward Frank, hacking repeatedly with the ax. He turned and saw Joe behind him. Dwight was now like a caged wild animal trying to escape his captors. The brothers felt helpless against his rage.

"Listen to me," Frank said. "Your name is Dwight Trilby. You're a student at Chartwell Academy in Kirkland. We are your friends. Can you repeat after me?"

Dwight staggered backward. "Tril— Tril—"

"That's it!" cried Joe. "Trilby!"

"Tril—byyyeeeaaahhhh!" At the sound of his own name, Dwight let out a hair-raising scream and turned on Joe.

There was no place to hide. As Dwight swung the ax, Joe grabbed his arm. The two of them struggled, each throwing the other off balance. Frank rushed over to help, but he couldn't pull Dwight away.

Thinking quickly, Joe stomped on Dwight's foot. Dwight howled and loosened his grip. Joe grabbed the ax from his hand. But Dwight reacted with twice as much fury. He clutched Joe's arm to try to get the ax back.

Joe tried to pull himself loose, but Dwight

pushed his arm downward, toward the floor near the water tank. Joe wouldn't let go of the ax.

Then, with a sudden, violent jerk, Dwight swung Joe's arm back up the other way. As Frank's eyes widened in shock, Joe went flying over the railing.

Chapter

15

"DWIGHT! NO!" FRANK shouted. But it was too late. Joe twisted desperately as he flipped into the air, still holding the ax.

The blade caught and hooked around a metal post that connected the railing to the walkway floor as Joe was falling. Amazingly the ax held, and Joe swung under the walkway, dangling from the ax handle.

Dwight saw this and grunted in anger. With his foot, he tried to unhook the ax blade from the post.

"Get him away, Frank!" yelled Joe.

Frank threw himself at Dwight. The two of them tumbled to the floor. The entire walkway shook as they wrestled.

Fighting Dwight was like fighting an octopus. His arms and legs flailed in unexpected ways.

I've got to get a grip on him, Frank thought. He swung himself around behind Dwight and tried to grab his neck. Dwight was caught unawares, but his elbow sailed up and landed a square hit on Frank's nose.

Next Frank went for Dwight's arms. He grabbed them tightly and tried to pin them down. But his grip loosened as Dwight kneed him in the stomach.

Meanwhile, behind Dwight, Frank could see Joe climbing slowly up the ax handle. He had just grabbed onto the post. If Frank could distract Dwight long enough, Joe would be back up on the walkway in a minute.

Frank leaped to his feet and assumed a wrestling position. "Come on, big guy, I dare you," he challenged. Dwight swung his fist wildly and Frank ducked. The force of Dwight's swing spun him around—just in time to see Joe lifting his leg onto the walkway.

"*Nyyyyaaaaahhhhh!*" Dwight cried as he ran toward Joe. He swept his foot across the walkway and kicked Joe's leg. Joe fell again, but this time he was hanging on to the railing.

The ax was still wedged between the railing and the floor. Dwight reached down and picked it up. He took aim at Joe's fingers and drew it back.

Thud! Just as Dwight was about to bring the ax down on Joe's hands, he crumpled to the walkway floor—Frank's karate blow had met its mark. The ax clattered to the metal floor beside Dwight.

Frank picked it up and sent it flying down into the trees below.

"Hang on, Joe!" Frank said.

"That's all I *can* do!" Joe replied through gritted teeth. His arms were beginning to weaken.

Frank hopped over Dwight and rushed to Joe. He grabbed Joe's arms below the wrists and pulled him up onto the walkway.

"Thanks, partner, you came through again," Joe said, massaging his arms. "Although I may have to buy shirts with longer sleeves from now on—"

"Feel strong enough to get Dwight back to campus?" Frank asked.

Joe gave him a weary look. "Let's go!"

Each took one end of Dwight and they walked clumsily down the spiral stairs, grunting under the strain.

"Not exactly petite, is he?" said Joe.

By the time they got to Chartwell's front gate, Dwight was upright and staggering. He had one arm around each Hardy.

"So—so—I jus' attacked you? Like—for n-n-no reason?" Dwight mumbled, slurring his words.

"Dwight, you were under the influence of whatever that masked guy sprayed in your face," Frank explained. He and Joe told Dwight what happened as they walked him to his room. They knocked on his door several times, until a sleepy roommate opened up.

"Yeah? Who is it?" He rubbed his eyes and saw Dwight, draped around Frank and Joe. "Oh, no, not another fight." He pulled Dwight inside, obviously used to his coming home in that condition.

As the door closed, the brothers looked at each other. "To the scene of the crime?" Joe asked.

Frank nodded.

They went out of the dorm and ran to the administration building. The door was just as they had left it. They entered the building and then climbed the stairs to the third floor. The door to the admissions office was open and the computer was still on.

"I'll look around for clues to the masked man's identity," said Joe.

"Okay," Frank said. "I'll cover up traces of our being here." He picked up the papers that Dwight had knocked onto the floor earlier. Then he went over to the computer. He saw the lit-up modem beside it.

"Maybe the masked man is an admissions official," he said to Joe.

"Could be. Can you dig up the personnel files on the computer?" Joe suggested.

"I'll try." Frank went over to the computer and looked at the screen. Columns of meaningless numbers shone back at him. He poised his fingers over the keys—

But just then, some of the numbers on the screen started to change.

"Joe! Look at this!" Frank said urgently. Joe rushed over to watch as a customer's ten-thousand-dollar account instantly dropped to five thousand dollars.

"They're stealing money *right now!*" Joe said. One by one, accounts began to decrease before their eyes.

"It's as if they're in a hurry to take as much as possible."

"As if they'd been discovered!"

"Joe, I just realized something! If they're doing this now, their phone line is open—"

"And we can trace the call from the van!"

Frank and Joe raced down the stairs and out to their van.

Frank took out the phone tracer and inserted the first three digits—555. All the Chartwell numbers began with that exchange.

Now to check which lines were busy. With a little luck only a couple would be engaged.

They couldn't be that lucky—only one number in the whole school was busy. 555-2301.

Frank shouted, "We've got it!"

"Terrific," said Joe, with a deadpan look. "So what do we do now? Call the number and ask their names?"

"No, we go back into the admissions office and look for a directory of school numbers."

Once safely inside, Frank's fingers flew over the computer keyboard. In seconds the screen glowed with two columns of numbers. On the left was a list of phone numbers, all beginning with 555. To the right of each number was a room number. Frank pressed the Page Down button repeatedly.

"Let's see—one-four-oh-oh—one-seven-oh-oh. Ah! Here we are—two-three-oh-one!"

Frank and Joe memorized the room number on the right-hand side: Ives C-42.

Just then the quiet was broken by the *whoosh* of a silenced gunshot. A flash of light cut through the room and chips of plaster fell from the ceiling. Frank and Joe hit the floor and scrambled out the door as another shot rang out.

"We can't leave through the front door with a sniper out there! We're sitting ducks!" Joe said as they raced down the hallway.

"There's one chance," Frank said. "Arnie once told me there is a system of tunnels connecting the buildings here. Let's hope I can find them now. And let's hope the gunman doesn't know about them, too! Come on—there must be an entrance in the basement."

They flew down the stairs to the basement. Before them stretched a long, dark, concrete tunnel. "Let's go!" shouted Frank.

The sound of their breathing echoed off the walls of the tunnel as they ran. Their feet splashed through puddles where water pipes had been slowly leaking.

At the end of the straight path, the tunnel forked. They went to the right and found that this tunnel was much smaller than the previous one. They had to crouch to avoid the pipes and cables that jutted down from the ceiling.

They stopped for a second to catch their breath and were aware of a sound behind them. Frank signaled for Joe to remain motionless. They heard running footsteps grow louder and louder. The sound came to an abrupt stop as the person reached the fork. After a moment the footsteps started again, but became softer and more distant.

"He went left!" whispered Joe. "Quick, let's find an exit!"

They followed the tunnel as it snaked around and then straightened off to the left. At the end of a long passageway was an exit sign. They ran toward it at full speed.

Next to the sign, a ladder led up to a metal trapdoor. Joe climbed up and pushed the door open, and Frank followed right behind. They closed the door behind them and saw that they were beneath the stands near the football field.

"We did it! Now let's get back to Mansfield!" Frank said.

But he spoke too soon. A bullet whizzed by them and ricocheted off a nearby pole. Frank and Joe took off at full speed. Obviously, their pursuer knew the tunnels better than they did.

Ten feet away was the athletic building. They ran behind it as another bullet knocked away a chunk of brick from the wall.

The Hardys kept running, and before long they were near Van Cott Hall. Light was streaming from the windows of the dorm's common room, and they could hear the faint beat of a rock song.

Frank and Joe ducked into the late-night party that was in celebration of no school the next day. There was a crowd of students there, dancing and singing to the music. By one of the walls was a long table with a bowl of punch and paper cups. Joe went over to get himself a cup and Frank followed, surveying the party.

In the middle of it all was Arnie, gyrating wildly and clumsily, his glasses on the verge of flying off his face. Brad was in a corner, talking smoothly with a girl. He caught a glimpse of Frank and slyly shot him a wink.

"Want some?" Joe asked Frank, holding a ladle full of punch.

Frank looked at the bowl. The thought of drinking citrus punch at a time like this turned his stomach. He looked back over the crowd. A couple of students he knew from his classes were there, as well as some teachers, including Mr. Osborn. Then Mr. Castigan walked through the open door and joined Mr. Osborn. Frank thought of trying to talk to him, but quickly decided it would be best not to draw attention to himself and Joe.

But Mr. Castigan noticed Frank and waved. Joe disappeared into the crowd to avoid being seen by him. Castigan smiled and clapped Frank on the shoulder, which surprised Frank since they hadn't parted as the best of friends. "You should try dancing!" he said with a wink. "It's better exercise than a basketball game!"

All Frank could think was that Castigan had decided to believe his story about the exam. Eventually Castigan moved on and Frank found Joe hiding behind a clump of people.

"Let's go," said Frank. "It's not safe for you in here. If Castigan catches you on campus, he'll kick us both out!"

Joe quickly grabbed another cup of punch, and the brothers slipped outside. They looked left and right and saw no one.

"I think we're safe, now," said Frank.

"Let's get over to your room and figure out what to do next," Joe suggested.

"Fine. It'll be empty for a while, and I think we should call Dad."

They went around the back of Van Cott Hall, taking a shortcut to Mansfield. As they rounded the brick wall that enclosed the garbage area, they broke into a run—and came face-to-face with the muzzle of a pistol!

Chapter

16

JOE'S LIGHTNING-QUICK reflexes took over. Without thinking, he flung his cup at the masked man. Citrus punch flew between the eye slits of his ski mask.

"Arrgghhh!" the man cried, temporarily blinded. As he drew his hands to his face, Frank and Joe took off.

Halfway across the courtyard, Frank stopped short. "Wait a minute, Joe," he said.

"What are you doing?" Joe demanded. "Let's get to Mansfield before this guy makes Swiss cheese out of us!"

"No. Come here!" Frank pulled his brother into the middle of the courtyard, toward the statue of George Howe Chartwell. They ducked behind the pedestal of the statue just as the masked man came out behind the back of Van Cott Hall.

In the darkness Frank and Joe could only see his silhouette, but they could tell that he was looking for them. They couldn't tell who he was when he took off his ski mask and trotted off toward Mansfield Hall.

"Just as I thought," said Frank. "He knows where I live. We can't go back there now. Who knows? He may even have a key!"

"You've got a point," Joe said. "But what's our next step?"

"Follow me." Frank led Joe back into Van Cott Hall. The party was just then starting to break up. Dozens of students milled around in the dorm's large front foyer. Frank and Joe plunged into the crowd.

"How can you think of partying at a time like this?" asked Joe, baffled.

"Just stay with me," Frank answered. "This is perfect; the foyer is too crowded for the guard to pay attention to us."

Frank kept an eye on the guard as more and more students filed into the foyer from the party. Then, as soon as the guard turned his back to talk to someone, Frank and Joe darted up the stairs toward the rooms.

"This is a girls' dorm," explained Frank. "They don't allow male visitors this late. That's why we had to sneak."

"Hmm, I suppose you're used to this sort of

thing by now," said Joe slyly as they walked down the second-floor hallway. Frank gave Joe a playful slap on the head and walked up to room 21.

He rapped softly on the door. There was no answer. Then he knocked a little louder.

"Who is it?" called a voice from inside.

"It's me, Sarah—Frank."

Sarah opened the door with a look of astonishment on her face. "How did you get up here?" she asked. Then she saw Joe. "Who's he?"

"Sarah, this is my brother, Joe." He grinned. "Don't mind the blond roots."

Joe turned red as he shook Sarah's hand, embarrassed. "It's supposed to wash out," he mumbled.

"Come on in," Sarah said, with concern in her voice. "My roommates are still at the dance. I was just doing some homework. Is something wrong?"

"It's a long story!" said Frank. "Can we use your phone?"

"Of course. You're not in danger, are you, Frank?"

"If you consider being chased by an armed wacko through the campus 'danger,' yes!" said Joe.

Sarah looked fearful as Frank made his call. "Hello, Dad? You've got to get over here, I think we've got the computer thieves—in action! It's Ives Hall, room C-forty-two. Got it? . . . As soon as you can get here—with police! We're heading over there right now! 'Bye!"

"Can you be on call in case we need you for anything, Sarah?" Frank asked. "We're on the brink of breaking this!"

"You know you can," she answered. "But why don't you wait till your father gets here?"

"Too long," said Joe. "The thieves may be done by that time. We should only need him for the clean-up."

With that, Frank and Joe ran down the stairs, sneaked back into the foyer crowd, and walked out the front door.

They looked all around the courtyard. There were no suspicious shadows. They tiptoed around to the back of Van Cott. No one was there.

Then, as fast as they could, they ran past Mansfield to its neighboring dorm, Ives Hall.

Ives was spooky looking, with tall, gabled roofs and narrow windows. Its deep red brick had become almost black with age, and there was a creaky wooden porch along the front of the building.

"This looks like a haunted house," said Joe. "And what are we going to tell *this* guard?"

"This is a boys' dorm," said Frank. "Just nod your head at the guard and look like you know where you're going!"

They both did just that, and the guard woke up from a catnap to nod back. They went up the stairs to the fourth floor.

"You'd think one of these buildings would have an elevator," Joe grumbled.

Frank ignored him and went ahead to find C-42. His eyes widened as he read the names on the door: "Goldman, Farnsworth, and Pierce."

"The three honchos at my tribunal!" Frank whispered as Joe read the names. "No wonder they wanted to expel me! *They're* doing the thefts!"

Muffled, agitated voices could be heard through the door. Frank and Joe put their ears against it to listen.

At first they had a hard time sorting out the sounds—hurried voices, computer noises, the sound of a phone hanging up—a modem—the closing of a window. But soon the voices became more distinct, and the brothers could make out snatches of whispered conversation:

"Let them get away?"

"I couldn't help it. They're more—"

"Found out where we are!"

"I knew we should never have gotten involved! We're all going to be expelled!"

"Where's *our* money?"

"Haven't we transferred enough by now—"

"No! We need a million—we're almost there!"

Joe turned to Frank and said, "Let's throw some excitement into their lives." He knocked on the door.

All at once the voices stopped. Joe knocked again. There was frantic shuffling inside.

"Who is it?" a very polite voice sang out.

"Subscription boys for the *Prison Gazette!*" Joe answered.

He was met by silence once again.

"Open up, fellas, unless you want to pay for a new door!" Joe said.

The door opened halfway. Ty Farnsworth peeked out. "Frank! I didn't recognize your voice!" he said. "That's a crazy sense of humor you have." He looked at Joe. "I don't believe we've met."

"We'll all have plenty of time to get to know each other," said Frank. "Mind if we step in?"

"Of course not," said Ty. He opened the door all the way. Frank and Joe walked in to see Lloyd and Stu lying casually on their beds, reading textbooks.

"Studying awfully late, aren't you?" said Frank. "I guess you have to squeeze your work in around bank swindles."

Lloyd rose calmly to his feet and gave Frank a puzzled smile. "That's a very strange joke, Frank. Are you feeling all right?" he asked.

"He's feeling a lot better than you'll be feeling behind bars!" said Joe.

Lloyd looked at his roommates, who both shrugged their shoulders. "I'm afraid you're making no sense. I'll have to ask you to—"

"Why don't I just spell it out for you, Pierce?" said Frank. "The three of you have learned that playing with computers can be profitable. For the past couple of weeks you've been using this computer to loot the Bayport Bank and Trust for hundreds of thousands of dollars, transferring them to some secret account. I admire you for catching on to me early. You tried to expel me, set my room on fire, forge my English exam, and then—"

"This is totally ridiculous!" said Lloyd.

"Is it? *You* told me you'd read my admissions essay, Lloyd—and you're in my English class. Who else would know what my handwriting looked like?"

All three roommates laughed. "And you, Goldman," Frank said, "you went after me with that oar, pretending it was because you were jealous. You probably couldn't care less about Sarah." Then he turned to Ty. "And was it *you*, Farnsworth, who took my roommate Arnie's key at the Young Turk the night of the fire?"

Stu and Ty both started to protest, but Frank cut them off. "And then, when the going was getting really rough, one of you put on a mask and tried to kill us off—as well as Dwight Trilby! I think you'll have a lot of explaining to do when the police get here. And you'd be wise not to try anything—assault and battery will just make it easier to convict you!"

Lloyd folded his arms thoughtfully. "I think the stress here at Chartwell has gotten to you and your friend, Frank. Maybe you should sit down with us and relax. Let me take your jackets."

Lloyd sauntered over to the closet and opened the door.

Frank and Joe were completely unprepared for what came next.

Out of the closet stepped a man—a man with a mask and a gun!

Chapter

17

FRANK AND JOE lifted their hands in the air. The masked man waved them over to the window with his gun. Frank and Joe obeyed. Then he continued waving.

"Y-you mean you want us to jump?" Joe said. He looked down on the blacktop three stories below.

The masked man nodded.

Lloyd Pierce began fidgeting. He looked over at Stu and Ty, who also seemed uncomfortable.

"Come on," Lloyd said to the man. "I thought you said no violence."

The man waved toward the window with even more conviction.

"Hey, hey!" said Stu, grabbing the masked man's arm. "If you do this, they'll blame the deaths on us! They'll say we pushed them!"

The mysterious man wrenched his arm loose. With one swift blow, he whacked Stu over the head with his pistol.

A hush fell over the room as Stu crumpled to the floor. Lloyd and Ty looked shocked.

"Uh—okay! J-just tell us what to do," said Ty. "And we'll do it—right, Lloyd?"

Lloyd was dumbfounded. Ty poked him roughly in the back. "Right, Lloyd?" Ty repeated.

"Oh!" Lloyd said, shocked back to reality. "Right! Anything you want!"

The masked man pointed to the window again with his gun and made a lifting motion.

"You want us to open the window?" Ty asked.

The man then pantomimed a push with his hands. "And then push them out?" said Lloyd, terrified. "Wait a minute—"

Ty was already walking over to the window. "Do what he wants, Lloyd!" he snapped. "He's got a gun!"

"There's got to be another way!" Lloyd said. He stepped forward to plead with the man, crossing in front of Frank and Joe.

That was all Joe needed. He grabbed Lloyd's outstretched arm and threw him into the masked man. The two of them fell onto the floor, and the man let loose a shot.

Thwoosh—Crack! The bullet whistled through the silencer and hit the computer. Sparks flew through the air and the masked man shielded his eyes. With lightning speed, Joe ripped the computer monitor out of its socket and hurled it at the man.

Both Lloyd and the masked man scrambled away as the heavy box flew toward them. Frank and Joe then headed for the door.

They heard the sound of crashing metal as they ran into the hallway. They bolted down the stairwell and out the front door, past the sleeping guard.

"Let's get as far away from here as we can!" yelled Frank.

"Nobody's tailing us!" Joe called out, looking over his shoulder.

"They will! Come on!"

Two shots sliced the air; one hit the ground near Joe's foot and the other dented a nearby metal Dumpster. Frank and Joe dove behind the Dumpster.

"Where are they?" Frank whispered.

Joe carefully stuck his head above the Dumpster. No one was in the courtyard, but he heard voices. He looked up to see three figures on a catwalk along the top of Ives Hall.

"They're on the roof!" Joe said.

"Ives is the tallest building on campus. They'll see us wherever we go!" said Frank.

"Have no fear." Joe picked up two large rocks and hurled them as far as he could. They rustled leaves and branches as they fell through the trees behind Ives.

Ty, Lloyd, and the masked man rushed to the other end of the catwalk. Two more muffled shots sounded, but farther away.

"Look at that! They think we're all the way over there!" said Frank, amazed.

"Sometimes the oldest tricks are the best," Joe replied with a grin.

"*That* sounds familiar," Frank said.

While the rooftop snipers were distracted, Frank and Joe quietly scurried away from school grounds.

After a while they reached residential streets in Kirkland and felt safely distant from campus. They sat on a curb.

"This is ridiculous," said Joe, looking around. "We're totally useless here. Let's wait a few minutes for the three of them to get off the roof and then go back!"

Frank shook his head, deep in thought. "Too risky," he said. "Besides, we've got to intercept Dad. Police or no police, he's not going to be expecting homicidal maniacs on a prep-school campus."

"Right! That's why I think we should go in and get the van!"

"No," said Frank evenly. "Better to let the van come to us."

Joe gave Frank a quizzical look. "What? Maybe you *are* cracking under the stress!"

"Don't forget—there's still someone on campus who's on our side."

"Sarah! Of course!"

"You catch on fast!" said Frank. "We'll call and ask her to drive the van here! Now all we have to do is find a phone."

They ran five blocks into the outskirts of downtown Kirkland. An old, abandoned gas station stood by the edge of a side street. The windows were boarded up and the pumps had rusted from lack of use—but the pay phone still worked.

Frank inserted a quarter and dialed. "Sarah, this is Frank—yes, I'm all right. I'm at the corner of Archer and Elliot in Kirkland, at an old gas station.

"Listen, can you drive our van over here? . . . There's a spare set of keys in a secret compartment near the steering wheel. It looks like a cigarette lighter, but just push it in three times and turn it twice to the right, and the keys will pop out. . . . As soon as you can! Don't waste a second. And don't let anybody see you!"

As they waited for the van, Joe paced back and forth. "This is a dumb idea, Frank! It'll take her forever to get here. We might as well walk—"

"Trust me," pleaded Frank.

Sure enough, within five minutes the van was speeding down Archer Street toward them at full throttle.

Frank and Joe ran into the street, waving their arms at the van. As the van raced closer, they motioned for it to pull into the gas station. But it didn't slow down.

138

Frank gestured broadly with his arms. "What is she doing?" he asked. The van veered into the left side of the road and headed straight for them.

"Look out!" screamed Frank. He and Joe jumped into the hedges by the road and the van missed them by inches. It swerved away from the gas pumps and screeched to a stop thirty yards down the road.

Frank and Joe sprang up from the ground as the van door opened.

Out stepped the masked man.

The color drained from Frank's face. "She betrayed us," he said.

Without saying another word, the brothers took off down Elliot Place. The road was unpaved, and it was quite narrow—too narrow for the van—as it wound into the woods. A wild shot passed through the branches of the trees above them as they flew along the dirt road.

Before long the trees gave way to a clearing. Frank and Joe found themselves running through a freshly cut field of grass. Now they were able to pick up the pace—until Frank tripped over a huge rock.

"Yeow!" he yelled as he rolled onto the ground. He looked over to see what had tripped him, and instantly he could tell where they were. The huge rock was a tombstone.

Frank picked himself up and ran after his brother, who was dodging tombstones left and right.

Behind them they could hear the heavy breathing of the masked man, in close pursuit. With a burst of speed, Frank and Joe ran past a marble statue and over a hill. On the other side was another section of the graveyard. This one was newer—there were several trucks around, and shovels and pickaxes littered the ground.

Another shot whizzed by them and shattered the window of a truck about five feet to the left of them. They ran sharply the other way—right into an open grave!

Joe's momentum pulled him over the grave, and he crashed to the ground on the other side. But Frank tumbled headfirst into the deep hole, hitting the bottom with a thud.

Joe tried to get up, but an agonizing jolt of pain shot up from his leg. His face twisted into a grimace as his sprained ankle buckled beneath him. He looked up to see the masked man standing on top of the hill with his hands on his hips. Grasping a shovel that was sticking out of a pile of dirt next to him, Joe forced himself to stand up.

"Don't bother," said the masked man as he walked steadily toward Frank and Joe. "How convenient—you've already chosen your plot. Looks like it's big enough for two. Shall we test it?"

He circled around the grave toward Joe, with his gun drawn. Joe tried to back away but fell again. He lay helplessly as the man stood directly above him. He pointed his gun at Joe and looked down into the grave.

"Hello, Frank," he said. The muffled voice sounded familiar to Frank, but the man was trying to disguise it by speaking in a growling bass whisper. "I wish you hadn't brought this on yourself, but you insisted on being nosy with the wrong person."

"Who are you?" snapped Frank. "At least you can give us that satisfaction before bumping us off!"

The masked man reared back his head and let out a deep-throated laugh. "I think it's *my* turn to be satisfied," he said. "Now, I'm sure you're thinking that I plan to shoot you here in cold blood." He grinned as he looked at the brothers' fearful faces. "But you're wrong. Why should *I* perform that nasty task when you can do it yourselves?" With that, he pulled the aerosol can out of his pocket. Joe was trapped.

Pressing his gun to Joe's throat, the man brought the aerosol to his prisoner's face. "Ever hear of pheromones? They're airborne chemicals that trigger emotions. Love—fear—rage—"

"Joe!" Frank yelled, but he could suggest nothing. One flick of the trigger and Joe would be history. Frank cringed as he watched the phero-mone spray waft around his brother. He knew which emotion this spray would bring—the same rage that had turned Dwight Trilby into a homicidal maniac—and Trilby had only gotten a brief taste of the spray.

The masked man smiled and backed away from Joe, still pointing the gun. "Now," he said. "Stand up."

Joe struggled to his feet, despite the injured ankle. "Pick that up," the man said, indicating the shovel. Joe obeyed.

By now the man had backed around to the other side of the grave. He cocked his gun. "Now, dig."

Frank and Joe both looked at him in disbelief.

"You heard me—*fill the hole!*" He fired a warning shot two feet above Joe's head.

"Do as he says, Joe!" Frank shouted.

Meekly, Joe threw a small shovelful of soil on top of Frank.

"Faster," the man commanded.

Joe dumped in some more soil.

"Faster!" The man was now screaming.

All of a sudden, it seemed that Joe had forgotten his ankle injury. His shovelfuls became larger. He picked up the pace of his digging, grunting with the effort.

"Excellent," the man said with sinister glee. He could see that the pheromones were taking effect.

Joe was now shoveling furiously, throwing mounds of dirt around Frank. Within ten minutes Frank was practically covered.

"Joe! Joe! Think of what you're doing!" Frank yelled.

But Joe was now foaming at the mouth. His eyes were rolling in their sockets, and he was babbling nonsense words.

Just as Frank was about to be covered, Joe began to shriek insanely. He backed away from the grave as if he were being attacked.

"Finish your job!" the masked man demanded.

But Joe was too far gone. He flailed his shovel around in midair, battling something that only he could see.

The masked man aimed his gun at Joe. "I was hoping not to do this, my friend, but you've failed me."

Bracing the gun with two outstretched arms, he fired.

Chapter

18

JOE DIDN'T SEE the flare of gunpowder from the shot. He didn't hear the bullet rip through the air toward his face.

And he didn't even feel the impact as it ricocheted off his shovel blade!

A red haze of rage had rolled in between him and the world. He swung the shovel violently and ran around in circles.

The masked man leveled his gun again and tried to follow Joe with his sights. "Stand still, you fool!" he snapped, his voice rising with frustration.

Joe's motions just became faster and jerkier. The masked man cocked his gun.

In blind rage, Joe howled and flung the shovel across the grave. The man dropped his gun as the shovel flew toward his face.

He ducked out of the way—but not in time. The shovel blade conked him on the side of the head.

He fell to the ground, unconscious.

Meanwhile, Frank had almost dug himself out from the grave. He looked around at his brother, who was now tearing around the graveyard, fighting with the tombstones.

Frank lifted his elbows up to the top of the soil. With a mighty heave, he pulled his body out of the dirt by pushing down with his arms.

Once free, he ran after Joe. "Joe!" he cried. "It's Frank! Your brother, Frank!"

Joe spun around and saw Frank running toward him. His eyes popped open and he howled again. He ran away from Frank, stopping to pick up any objects he could throw: shovels, pickaxes, rocks. The objects flew toward Frank, and he kept ducking away.

Joe kept running until he reached a parked truck. He climbed inside and began pushing and pulling knobs, trying to start the engine. Frank reached the truck just as Joe accidentally turned on the radio full-blast.

Reacting to the sound of a blaring heavy-metal band, Joe flung himself out of the other side of the truck and began pulling at his hair. He lurched around spastically to the music, gouging himself as if trying to pick off invisible animals from his skin.

"Joe! Calm down! Listen to me!" Frank

pleaded. He tried to grab Joe but couldn't get a grip. As the music moved faster and faster, Joe's motions became more and more violent.

Frank climbed into the truck to turn off the radio. But all that was left of the On/Off switch was a hole where Joe had pulled it out. Frank banged on the radio, but it was no use.

It was hopeless. Frank closed his eyes and bellowed at the top of his lungs: "Stop it, Joe! You're going to kill yourself!"

Suddenly a spark flew out of the radio. *Dzzzzit!* The song stopped, and Joe collapsed in a heap on the ground.

Frank jumped out of the truck and ran to his brother. Joe's pulse was normal; Frank breathed a sigh of relief. From behind him came the sound of voices. He looked back to see two familiar figures walking over the hill toward him—Jed Wilson and Malcolm Rogers! In Rogers's hand was an Electrojam.

"Is he going to be all right?" Rogers asked.

"I think so," said Frank. "Thanks to you."

Mr. Rogers smiled. "Don't thank me, thank your friend Jed. He heard the music from way out on Archer Street!"

"But how—I thought—" Frank stuttered.

"I know, you can't understand why I'm here with Jed after the treatment I gave you at my apartment last week!"

"I thought you wanted to kill me! You *did* shoot at me, after all."

"I may have been suspicious of you, but I didn't want to kill you. My gun went off by accident—and I forgot that I had told Oscar to load it! I was as shocked as you when it fired.

"You see, when I saw you snooping around my papers that night, I thought *you* were the one who stole the money from the bank. I tried to tail you several times on campus, as you know. But then I saw Sedgwick Trilby's son this evening, and he told me all about you. I decided then that I wanted to work *with* you."

"Then how did you find me here?" Frank asked. He looked at Jed. "And how did you two end up together?"

"I saw you guys acting strange at the party," Jed said. "So I watched you after you left. All of a sudden there was this gunfire. I saw it from my room. Everything got quiet for a while, but then I saw your van tear out. So I ran out to my car to follow."

"And when *I* saw your van go, I thought I'd catch up with you to make friends," said Rogers. "But I lost track of the van. Then I noticed Jed was behind me. I recognized his old jalopy as the one from which I took an Electrojam the other night by the boathouse. So I stopped him. He explained Electrojam; I explained the bank thefts; and we joined forces."

Just then Joe began to stir. As he struggled to open his eyes, he came face-to-face with Mr. Rogers.

Joe shuddered. "Is *that* the masked dude?" he asked.

Frank sprang to his feet. "Wait a minute," he said, looking at Mr. Rogers. "You're obviously not the masked man!"

"Only at a Halloween ball, my friend," Rogers said.

"Then who is *that?*" Frank pointed to the man who still lay where Joe's shovel had knocked him out. "Who is the man that tried to kill us?"

Frank, Joe, and Mr. Rogers ran over to the mysterious man. Joe straggled behind, holding his aching head. The man was beginning to stir and groan.

When the four of them were gathered around, Frank pulled off the man's ski cap. He and Joe both gasped.

It was Jim Castigan.

"I can't believe it!" Frank said almost to himself.

Mr. Rogers shook his head. "I hate to say it, but I can."

"You know Mr. Castigan?" asked Joe.

"I *employed* him," said Rogers. "Years ago, this man couldn't get a job. Brilliant chemist and computer programmer, but it seemed he had sticky fingers. He stole money and chemicals from several of the companies he worked for. Trying to finance some weird research into pheromones."

"I think he finally succeeded," said Joe, wincing with pain.

Mr. Rogers continued, "He worked in the research and development department of a computer company I used to run. He shaped up, and helped develop all sorts of new programs for us."

"Including the one that Bayport Bank and Trust bought!" Joe said.

Rogers paused thoughtfully. "Now that you mention it, that's very possible," he said. "At any rate, Castigan left the company to pursue his teaching career, and I understand he had a spotless record."

"Until now," said Frank.

"Too bad his greed had to suck in Lloyd and Ty and Stu," said Joe.

Frank hung his head. "And Sarah," he said softly.

For a moment, no one knew what to say. But the tense silence was broken by the sound of footsteps coming over the hill.

"Okay, don't panic! We've got you covered."

They looked up to see two policemen jogging toward them with guns drawn. Behind them was Fenton Hardy. Frank and Joe looked at each other and exploded into laughter.

"Just in time, Dad," said Frank.

Fenton and the policemen handcuffed Castigan, and they all walked back out to the road.

Back at the campus, as the police rounded up

Pierce, Goldman, and Farnsworth, Frank paid a visit to Van Cott Hall. He sneaked in through an open window, walked to the second floor, and knocked on room 21.

"Stu?" Sarah asked softly through the door.

"No," Frank replied.

"Jim!" she said excitedly, and pulled the door open. Her smile gave way to a shocked expression when she saw Frank. "Gin—Ginny! I thought you were my friend Ginny!" she said, trying to cover up.

"It's no use, Sarah. It's all over, the whole thing. The police have Castigan, and they're about to come up to take you in for questioning."

Sarah frowned and started to close the door. "You know it's awfully late, Frank. How did you get in here, anyway?"

Frank stuck his foot in the door. "Please just tell me one thing," he said. "Why did you do it? How could someone as smart as you get mixed up with a criminal like Jim Castigan?"

Sarah's hair fell in front of her face as she looked down. A tear rolled off her cheek. She let the door open.

"He was so smart," she said. "And so attractive. Even you have to admit what a magnetic teacher he is. And he promised us everything. He was going to take care of us all—if we helped him out.

"He convinced us that you only get what you

want by outwitting everybody else and only taking from those who can afford the loss.

"See, Lloyd and Stu and Ty—and me—we're all scholarship students. Do you know what it's like to be with all these rich kids, year after year, when you have nothing? Jim understood that."

Sarah sighed. "He called himself a modern Robin Hood. That's why he took only from a wealthy bank."

"And you believed that?"

Sarah nodded sadly. "We all did. And he rewarded us. He gave us all A's in chemistry. Then he promised us enough money to set us up for life, and he guaranteed no one could ever trace it."

The sound of policemen's footsteps echoed in the stairwell behind them. "Well," said Frank with a sigh, "he was wrong."

As the policemen came to take Sarah to the station house, Frank walked slowly away.

Frank and Joe watched as Jim Castigan, Lloyd Pierce, Stu Goldman, Ty Farnsworth, and Sarah Waterbury were escorted into squad cars and driven away.

Fenton walked up to them. "Amazing story," he said. "The guy had dreams of his own little world, a high-tech paradise with no financial problems. His lifeline to the real world would be a paid group of young geniuses who served his every wish.

"It almost worked," said Fenton as he walked to his car. "But he didn't know who he was up against." He winked. "See you at home, boys."

Frank turned to Joe as their father drove off. "You want to know the truth? I am *not* going to miss being a student at Chartwell."

"You mean you're not going to finish out the semester at least?" Joe said in mock horror.

Frank chuckled. "No way. *And* I think I'll destroy every reminder of this place." He reached into his side pocket and pulled out an Electrojam. "Including this."

As Frank walked toward the Dumpster, the squeal of tires cut through the still night air. An old sedan spun around the administration building, barreling right toward Frank and Joe.

"Look out!" yelled Frank. He and Joe hurled themselves behind the Dumpster.

The sedan screeched to a halt. Music blasted from its huge speakers.

"OH, BABY, BABY, PLEASE LET ME BE! OH, YEAH! OH, NO!"

"I know who that is," grumbled Frank.

"Hey, Frank! Is that you?" Arnie called from his open window. "I snuck out. I can't get to sleep, either! Want to go for a ride? Where are you?"

Joe gave Frank a sidelong glance. "Now?" he whispered.

"Now," his brother answered, handing Joe the Electrojam.

Dzzzzit.

Once again, the night was silent. "Hey, what happened to my new CD player?" Bewildered, Arnie turned his full attention to his dashboard.

"If we split now," Frank said, "we'll get to Bayport in time to sleep part of the night in our own beds."

"We're out of here!" said Joe. "You lead the way!"

With smiles of triumph on their faces, Frank and Joe slipped into the night.

Frank and Joe's next case:

A staged hijacking is just role-playing, until things go terribly wrong. Real terrorists have seized the plane. Still worse, Callie Shaw, Frank's girlfriend, is aboard!

There's only one slim lead that may bring the Hardys to the terrorists' commander, a shadowy figure known only as the Dutchman. But can they reach the Dutchman in time? Find out in *Hostages of Hate*, Case #10 in The Hardy Boys Casefiles.